Bible Basics

An Essential Guide to the Book of Genesis

Sean Purcell

Bible Basics: An Essential Guide to the Book of Genesis

First published in 2024 by

Annunciation Press
East Bridge House, East Street, Colchester, Essex, CO1 2TX
hello@annunciation.press

Book layout by Annunciation Press

To Noah, who has the ability to bring both rest and motion to our lives.

Acknowledgments

I'd like to thank my family for their support whilst I completed this book, particularly when I locked myself away for long periods of time to make sure that everything was correct and accurate, missing out on key family moments. Your continued support for me and my projects is never undervalued.

I want to also thank my GCSE RE students for inspiring me to write this book. When I first began teaching them, they were dismissive of the value and need for Religious Education in their lives, but I hope that I have inspired them enough to see that RE is a fundamental subject that impacts their lives in ways they may never fully comprehend. Their attempts to learn about the Book of Genesis (and my attempts to teach it), led me to wonder why there wasn't a fairly short and simple introductory book on such an important topic, which in turn led to this project...so Year 10s, I have you to blame for embarking on this adventure!

Finally, I want to thank you for purchasing this book and reading it. I hope that you find it interesting and thought-provoking, and if that happens for you then I will have fulfilled my objective.

Contents

Introduction

**"Although no one can go back and make a brand-new start,
anyone can start from now and make a brand-new ending."**

— Carl Bard

New Beginnings. A fresh start.

The concept inspires all of us, whether it's a transformation story
of someone we believe in, love, or ourselves. Everyone plateaus,
everyone regresses, everyone wants to reinvent their lives at
some point. We love the idea of change, whether it's witnessing a
weight loss journey, a substance abuser who finds sobriety, a
rags-to-riches philanthropist, a complete home renovation, or a
relationship rekindling love long lost. It warms the heart. It kicks
us into gear. It motivates us.

So, what does a fresh start have to do with *Bible Basics:
Genesis*? If you have any background studying the Bible, you
might know the word translates to "creation," specifically "in the
beginning." God created the universe, and in the same way we
love transformation stories, God continues to create new people

like you from old lives and habits. God, too, loves new beginnings.

Let me introduce myself as the author, Sean, by saying, "Welcome. I'm glad you're here."

I don't know where you're at in your spiritual journey if you picked this up completely new to the subject or are engaged in academic study to be a subject matter expert.

If new to the subject, you might see the Bible as just another book, albeit maybe an important one. It might be in an unused cupboard at your house that's never been read past a couple of chapters. Perhaps it was discussed in your religious studies class, or you traditionally attend mass for Christmas and Easter. You might be vaguely familiar with the characters and concepts in the Bible, but leave the rest for the clergy to know and study. It's confusing, right? The context, the characters, the theology, the big words and concepts that fly right over your head.

I agree with you. The Bible is not an easy read by any means. With so many layers to unpack, can you ever fully understand it? Or God? A renowned theologian, St. Augustine of Hippo, once said, "If you understood him, it would not be God."

So, why should you read this book? How can this book benefit your life? It will equip you to personally interact with God as you read through His word. Wherever you are in your spiritual journey, the Bible is packed with lessons to be interpreted and applied, whether it's faith, hope, morals, purpose, mission, calling, or relationships,

The words come to life when your heart stirs for the God who wrote them. I've come to know God through the Bible, but God is so much more than just a book. He is eternal, alive, and active, able to transform hearts. If you're looking for a new beginning,

Introduction

consider God as the catalyst to your transformation alongside the Bible and this book as a guide.

As with any story, the first page of Genesis 1:1 is a great place to start. "In the beginning, God created the heavens and the earth." *Bible Basics* is a series that answers the most pertinent questions and topics in the Bible. Whether you're just curious or engaged in academic study, *Bible Basics* will teach you to interpret God's Word by providing the context in which it was written.

As a part of our study, we will look at some of the following aspects:

Chapter 1: In the Beginning

- Genesis placement and role in the Bible, and how it applies to your life thousands of years later.

Chapter 2: Adam and Eve

- The account of Genesis, Adam and Eve, and their relationship with God before and after the "Fall."

Chapter 3: Cain and Abel

- In the first murder, Cain murders his brother Abel, envious of God's favoured treatment of Abel.

Chapter 4: Noah and the Flood

- The story of Noah and the Flood tells how the wickedness of humankind leads to the erasing of all human life besides Noah's family.

Introduction

Chapter 5: Tower of Babel

- The role of the Tower of Babel and God's decision to disperse humanity throughout the earth, confusing the builders by introducing different languages.

Chapter 6: Abraham

- Abraham's journey of faith as the father of what became the Israelite nation from the land of Ur to Canaan and Egypt and back to Canaan.

Chapter 7: Sarah and Hagar

- The relationship between the two women and the complexity of family in the Ancient Near Eastern context.

Chapter 8: Jacob and Esau

- How God decides to bless the younger brother Jacob and have the older brother Esau serve Jacob.

Chapter 9: Joseph

- Joseph, the favoured son of Jacob, is taken advantage of by his brothers and sold into slavery in Egypt.
- The reconciliation between Joseph and his brothers and the restoration of Jacob's family

Introduction

Chapter 10: The Twelve Tribes of Israel

- The twelve tribes of Israel developed from a family into a nation ultimately led by Moses to the Promised Land of Canaan.

Chapter 11: Themes of Covenants in Genesis

- The importance of God's covenants and their fulfilment throughout the Bible, including the Noahic, Abrahamic, and Mosaic covenants.

Chapter 12: Genesis and Its Influence on World Religions

- How Genesis plays a role in Judaism, Christianity, and Islam and acts as a foundation for interfaith dialogue.

God has played an intimate role in shaping history. His ultimate goal? To redeem humanity. The Fall's effects can be felt world-wide - death, pain, and natural disasters - but God promises to make it right. To change a heart like yours, one at a time, and ultimately redeem the world to experience eternal life. This may be the book that shows you that for the first time.

Chapter 1
In the Beginning

"It is no accident that *God* is the subject of the first sentence of the Bible, for this word dominates the whole chapter and catches the eye at every point of the page."

— Derek Kidner

"In the beginning, God created the heavens and the earth."

— Genesis 1:1

Although only ten words, Genesis' opening verse summarizes one of the most important truths - the introduction of God's creation and His sovereignty over time. God made the heavens and the earth from no other source but His own creative power.

Creation Myths Across Different Cultures.

Although we will focus on the biblical account of creation, let's also look at the period in which Genesis was written. Scholars attribute the likely author of Genesis to Moses, the leader of the

Israelites, who brought them out of slavery in the land of Egypt to Canaan, the "Promised Land." Scholars believe Genesis was written around 1,400 B.C. During that period, cultures across the globe developed cosmological narratives of the universe's origins based on their unique beliefs, values, and understanding.

Genesis was written during the Ancient Near East, home of the early human civilizations in what is now the Middle East, Turkey, Egypt, and parts of North-eastern Africa, spanning 5,000 BC-700 AD. One of the early civilizations, Mesopotamia, believed in a creation narrative known as the Enuma Elish, the Babylonian myth describing how the gods created the world from primordial chaos.

The Ancient Egyptians believed in similar versions of events - the Heliopolitan myth - claiming the oldest of their ancient gods Atum, created the world. Egyptians also believed in the Memphite myth, postulating that the creator deity, Ptah, brought the world into existence by thinking and speaking it.

Why So Important? Theological Interpretations of Genesis 1:1

Although just one verse, many scholars, theologians, believers, and cultures widely interpret Genesis 1:1. Most acknowledge God created the heavens and the earth "ex nihilo," or out of nothing. How he specifically created the earth over what period is what differs amongst the church.

The literal view of how long it took for creation is that Genesis 1:1 is, as it reads, a precise timeline, referring to a 6-day creation consisting of 24 hours each day. Those who interpret Genesis 1:1 from the literal view believe in a young earth creation story, stating the earth is anywhere from 6,000 to 10,000 years old, dated predominantly from biblical genealogy and documented historical events.

The Day-Age interpretation believes that the six days in Genesis 1 actually refer to a period greater than 24 hours, known as an "age" or "epoch." Day-age interpreters attempt to complement modern scientific findings that the earth is older than 6,000-10,000 years old.

The Gap theory postulates that a space in time existed between Genesis 1:1 and 1:2. According to the theory, God created a perfect earth for an indefinite time until a catastrophic event occurred between verses one and two. Gap theorists propose the catastrophic event could be the rebellion of Lucifer and the fallen angels against God and the angels described in Revelations 12:7-10. Gap theorists argue this could have caused the earth to retrograde from a state of perfection to "formless and void," needing recreation from Genesis 1:2 onward.

The framework interpretation believes the creation argument's focus should be on God's sovereignty and His purpose for Creation rather than the actual events and processes. It interprets Genesis more as a literary structure written to exemplify God's power, not to demonstrate its historical accuracy.

Theistic Evolution or Evolutionary Creationism believes God used microevolution and macroevolution to bring about every animal, life, and system into existence. They therefore attempt to incorporate the narrative of creation with evolution,

What Was It Like? The Historical Context of the Ancient Near East.

The Ancient Near East contained unique beliefs and social structures that can make Genesis challenging to understand if one has never studied the religions of that period. The Ancient Near Eastern religions incorporated cosmology and creation stories, common polytheistic belief systems, a temple cosmology focus, priests, and symbolism.

Mesopotamia, Egypt, and Canaan believed in hundreds of gods representing different aspects of human existence and watching over the affairs of man. Ancient Near Eastern religions prayed to the gods for blessings (like a fertile season of crops) and curses upon their enemies (when engaged in war).

Temples used throughout the Old Testament were integral to Ancient Near Eastern religions - they were links to the cosmos and a way to connect with the divine. God related himself to the Israelites at that time in how they understood spiritual worship, instituting temples as part of their religion.

Priests were seen as officiators and intermediates between God and man. They conducted acts of worship to God to atone for the sins of the people, including themselves.

Ancient Near Eastern civilizations often adopted gods from other civilizations into their religion. Genesis directly conflicted with other Ancient Near Eastern religions, clearly stating only God created the heavens and the earth. The Old Testament describes how God fought on behalf of the Israelites to prove that He alone was God.

What Are Some Overarching Themes?

Genesis describes a God who exists, who is all-powerful, a God of order and structure who wants what is ultimately good, portraying Him as intentional, that He created man with a unique role of stewardship, and made man and woman in His image.

Genesis: The Foundational Text.

Genesis acts as a foundational text, stating the origins of creation, introducing key theological themes, following the covenantal narrative of some of the main characters of the Old Testament, giving an understanding of human nature and sin, and explaining the theological significance and continuity of the bible's entire narrative.

Genesis looks at the broadest aspects of creation, getting more specific each day and focusing on creating humanity the sixth day. It answers the most critical questions. How, why, and where do we exist?

We learn about God's sovereignty, humanity's nature, the effects of sin, the promise of redemption, the binding power of a covenant, and the promise of salvation.

What Does Everyone Have to Say About It? Contemporary Debates.

Genesis is vastly debated in contemporary circles. Its influence reaches history, science, theology, and ethics, to name a few. One of the most widely discussed topics about Genesis revolves around creation versus evolution. Evolution catapulted onto the world stage after the famous Scopes Monkey Trial in 1925, a renowned case about a teacher who illegally taught evolution in Dayton, Tennessee.

During the trial, defence attorney Clarence Darrow famously cross-examined prosecuting attorney William Jennings Bryan. Darrow questioned Bryan's interpretation of Genesis and his views on cosmology, making him appear uneducated and irrational to the whole world. It seemed like Genesis was on trial... and it lost, at least in the eyes of the world. Since then, evolution has become the consensus scientific theory on cosmology. Genesis and creationism have recently gained more attention, however. Scientists continue to find discrepancies in the theory of evolution that fall short of explaining the universe's origins conclusively.

Chime In Religious Scholars. Early Interpretations of Genesis.

The Jews widely debated whether the account of Genesis was an allegory or a literal series of events. In the first century CE, Philo of Alexandria proposed the interpretation of Genesis as an allegory, blending Jewish culture and Greek philosophical thought. Another school of thought, Rabbinic Midrashim, used allegorical methods to interpret Genesis, filling the gaps in the biblical narrative with imaginative stories and ethical teachings.

Origin and Augustine, amongst many early Christian church fathers, viewed the creation story as symbolic and significant rather than a literal reading with historical accuracy. Medieval Christian commentators such as John Calvin and Thomas Aquinas focused on the significance of the narrative rather than the sequence of Creation itself, writing in their commentaries about God's sovereignty, human nature, sin, and redemption.

Let's Compare Genesis's Account With Other Ancient Near Eastern Religions.

Ancient religions believed in diverse creation processes, either a single deity, a world of gods, mythical creatures, or cosmic sacrifices producing the universe. They debated whether the cosmos came from chaos or order, whether it developed from the separation of elements or the power of a god/gods.

Although Genesis and other religious narratives differ on creation, there are some fundamental themes or similarities between them. Their creation narratives all attempt to explain the origins of humanity, how they relate to the divine and their purpose in the world.

Light and Darkness: Genesis.

Light is the first element that God creates. Why? Because He is light, described in 1 John 1:5. Light symbolizes truth, righteousness, goodness, and divine illumination, revealing things as they are. Light reflects His power, bringing about order in the universe.

The Spirit of God's Role In Creation.

Translated as the "wind" or "breath" of God, the Spirit of God is actively involved in God's creation. Genesis 1:2 states how the Spirit of God was

"hovering over the waters."

The word "hovering" or "moving" implies that a divine agency (the Spirit) was preparing the expanse for God's creative action. The Spirit of God is present amid emptiness and voidness, demonstrating that He can prepare any "without" or "chaotic" area for new creation.

The Spirit of God reflects God's divine immanence and transcendence. He is present throughout His Creation yet separate from the Creation itself.

The Seventh Day. Rest.

God's rest on the seventh day highlights the completion of creation, acting as a model for rest and a symbol of covenant and blessing between humanity and Him.

God's rest is also a model for the Israelites, honouring the sabbath as a holy day of rest, reflection, and worship. God gave humanity a model to follow, to rest from work for physical and spiritual rejuvenation, helping people to acknowledge their dependence on God rather than their efforts and to commune with God on a deeper level.

Sean Purcell

Allegorical Interpretations of The Creation Story.

Many values and themes can be drawn from allegories found in creation.

The Garden of Eden symbolizes paradise, a perfect communion with God and nature, representing harmony, innocence, and peace. It gives a picture of the new heavens and new earth God promises to create in Revelations 21.

Adam can be interpreted as a symbol of the human condition and its pitfalls; Eve as a symbol of femininity.

The Tree of Knowledge and the Forbidden Fruit are archetypes of free will, good versus evil, and humanity's ability to decide between right and wrong.

The Serpent is an archetype for the reality of temptation, what leads people to do, say, and think evil and stray from God's moral truths and commands.

The Relationship between Faith and Reason in Genesis.

Faith and reason both play a role in one's experience of God. Just as faith in Genesis describes that God created the universe in all its complexity, reason convinces one that an intelligent Being (God) created the order within the universe. Although often viewed this way, faith and reason are not always antagonistic. Both can complement a person's beliefs in God.

Faith and reason demonstrate the limitations of human reasoning and the perfection of God's knowledge. Human reasoning falls short of determining all the consequences of one's decision. For example, Adam and Eve didn't comprehend that their decision would forever alter their lives and people throughout history. They were merely told to trust God despite their own reasoning. Many characters in the Bible learn to believe God over their assumptions. Emotions, lack of foresight, and complexities can all blind human reason.

What Do the Wise Guys Think? Theological and Philosophical Concepts.

Ontology, teleology, metaphysics, ethics, and epistemology appear indirectly in Genesis. Let's look at them briefly.

Ontology attempts to answer:

Who are we, and how we exist?

Genesis answers: we exist because God created us.

Teleology attempts to answer the question:

Why are we here? What purpose do we serve?

Genesis answers: we have a purpose because God created us to love Him and love others.

Metaphysics attempts to answer the question:

What is really real? How do we know we exist?

Genesis answers: God defines reality. Time, matter, and space all exist because of Him.

Ethics attempts to answer:

What is right from wrong?

Genesis answers: obey God in faith because His ways are higher than ours.

Epistemology attempts to answer:

How do we know what we know? How do we gain or acquire knowledge?

Genesis answers: human reason is limited. We understand whatever has been revealed to us.

What Makes Genesis 1 Stand Out? Literary Devices.

Several literary devices contribute to Genesis' impactful narrative style.

Parallelism: the phrase "And God said…and it was so" is used throughout the first chapter, affirming the rhythmic structure of God's creative process.

Refrains and Repetition: the refrain "And there was evening, and there was morning" repeats after each day of creation, providing a framework to signal the completion of each creative act.

Imagery and Metaphor: Genesis incorporates imagery and metaphors. "God's Spirit hovering over the waters" gives a more vivid picture of Creation.

Anthropomorphism: Genesis 1 uses human-like characteristics to describe God's actions. "God saw that it was a good" compares God's ability to evaluate to humans' ability to evaluate.

Time and Genesis 1.

Genesis marks the beginning of the sequential, structured framework, time.

Time is separated between light as day and darkness as night. Time is evaluated by 24-hour periods separated by light and dark, typically around 12 hours of daylight and 12 hours of darkness - varying depending on the season and part of the world. Time is evaluated in sequential order, distinct days, and is cyclical, repeating days, months, and seasons throughout the year.

Bible Basics

God creates time in Genesis but lives outside of it, existing eternally at every moment of history, before the world's beginning and after its end.

Ex Nihilo.

Although the word is not translated directly from the Bible, ex nihilo, literally meaning "out of nothing," refers to God's creation of the universe out of thin air. The Hebrew word "bara" refers to "created" in Genesis 1:1, meaning God created the universe independently without effort from any other being or using matter.

Art and Literature. Genesis' Impact.

The depiction of creation, the Garden of Eden, and the biblical figures of Adam, Eve, Noah, and Abraham have been recounted in paintings and drawings spanning millennia - incorporated in stained glass windows in churches, synagogues, religious institutions, and sculptures, paintings, and frescoes.

Some famous examples of literary works influenced by the stories, themes, and moral lessons found in Genesis include

1. "Paradise Lost" by John Milton
2. "East of Eden" by John Steinbeck
3. "The Book of Sand" by Jorge Luis Borges
4. "The Red Tent" by Anita Diamant
5. "The Children of Men" by P.D. James
6. "The Last Temptation of Christ" by Nikos Kazantzakis:
7. "The Robe" by Lloyd C. Douglas
8. "The Handmaid's Tale" by Margaret Atwood

I Care About It. God's Creation.

God bestows humans as caretakers or stewards of the natural world (Genesis 1:26-28). Genesis 2:15 highlights the importance of cultivating (working the land) and keeping (protecting or persevering it) the earth as stewards. The Garden of Eden is seen as the ideal state of the world, lush with plants, trees, and diverse ecosystems that were preserved by God's hand. God's original intention for the earth? To be beautiful, harmonious, balanced, sustainable, and preserved.

Rest Up. The Concept of the Sabbath.

In the biblical sense, rest means much more than the physical aspect of sleep. Although sleep plays a vital role in one's rest throughout the week, the Sabbath refers to an emotional, mental, and spiritual rest, reflecting on God's goodness, restoring our minds, bodies, and spirits, and rejuvenating ourselves for the coming week.

Different Religious Traditions. What Do They Say?

According to the Midrashic interpretation, Jewish tradition searches for deeper meanings in the text outside of the literal events of creation. Judaism views Genesis in the context of God's covenant with Abraham and the Israelites.

Christianity focuses heavily on creation, original sin, and the symbolic/moral teachings in the text. Christians emphasize that Genesis establishes the context of the human condition and the need for a Saviour to redeem humanity from their sin.

Islam views Genesis as an important religious text but differs widely in its interpretation. Islam recognizes Adam as a vicegerent of God or a ruler delegated authority by God to steward the Earth. Noah, Abraham, and Moses are prophets in

Islam as examples of obedience to God and an essential link to the prophetic lineage.

The Role of Faith in Understanding Genesis.

As anyone approaches Genesis, faith plays a role in interpreting the Bible. One must believe in divine revelation, that God can communicate with people throughout history, that in fact He has communicated with people throughout history, and that His plan is redemptive.

Conclusion.

To truly transform in your relationship with God, you have to attach significance to His Word, believe in the authority of the Scripture, and study it. The more weight the words carry, the more they apply to your life, the more you change as an individual.

Your prior experiences, worldview, and previous interaction(s) with the Bible will significantly impact your interpretation of it. Your community, upbringing, and personal convictions impact your pursuit of understanding the Bible.

We hope your interest in the Bible has grown in what it says about God and you as His creation.

In the next chapter, we will discuss Adam and Eve, the role of the serpent in their temptation, and God's response to their disobedience. We'll study themes of free will, consequences of sinful decisions, redemption, and God's intention behind the creation of humanity.

Chapter 2
Adam and Eve

"The tree was to be desired for the sake of nourishment, not of prohibition. And this is confirmed by what follows, for God said: 'Behold, Adam is become as one of us, knowing good and evil.' Thereafter he is banished from the tree lest he should live forever in his sins."

— St. Augustine

"So God created mankind in his own image, in the image of God, he created them; male and female he created them."

— Genesis 1:27

If only it was easy enough to blame Adam and Eve for all the world's problems. After all, eating from the Tree of Forbidden Fruit was THEIR choice, leading to OUR temporal separation between God and His creation. Death, pain, and natural disasters we see come as a result of one fateful decision.

Bible Basics

Why would one mistake cause so much evil?

Sin has devastating consequences. As used to it as we are, sin is a heinous crime in the eyes of God, rejecting His very nature. It deserves death and eternal separation from him. Thankfully, God is forgiving, slow to anger, and abounds in love. God is able to forgive everything we've ever done, everything we continue to do, and everything we will ever do - on one condition. Belief in His Son Jesus Christ.

Jesus? What does Jesus have to do with me?

Jesus is God who took on the form of a physical body, lived a perfect life, yet was tempted and tried as we are in every possible way, then died on the cross to take our sins upon himself, resurrecting from the grave 3 days later so that we might have eternal life with Him. He did so that you could be free from your guilt and shame and live a new life marked by joy, peace, and love.

Let's now look at Adam and Eve and how their decision led to long-lasting consequences only God could redeem through His Son Jesus.

You Had One Job. Adam and Eve's Role in The Garden.

In Genesis 2, Adam is given the authority to name every animal as a ruler of the earth. God noticed Adam was alone in the Garden without a suitable partner. God decides to make a "woman from the rib he had taken out of the man," presenting Eve before Adam when he wakes up from deep slumber. Adam proclaims that Eve is "bone of my bone and flesh of my flesh," representing his companionship and compatibility with Eve. They are united as "one flesh," the bond between a husband and a wife. Adam and Eve were instructed to enjoy paradise on one condition. Don't eat the forbidden fruit. The consequences? Death.

Made in the Image of God?

Genesis 1:26-27 brings up a concept with significant theological implications - humans are "made in the image of God."

What does this mean, exactly? Humans reflect God's divine attributes: the capacity for relationships, spirituality, creativity, morality, rationality, and intellect. No other creature is capable of all these aspects.

As a result of the Fall, humanity's reflection as image-bearers of God was corrupted. However, humanity still has redemptive potential, meaning God can fully restore our reflection as humans made the image of God.

The Gravity of Sin. Adam and Eve's Disobedience.

Adam and Eve were given perfection, just instructions and one warning. Do not eat the forbidden fruit. One warning. It was that easy!

Eve, led by curiosity and temptation, stood before the Tree of Knowledge, listening to the serpent luring her into eating the fruit. Eve saw the fruit looked appealing to the eye and believed the serpent when he said it would make her and Adam like God. The serpent failed to mention the true consequences of their disobedience. Adam and Eve trusted the serpent and their own desires over God's. Billions of lives lost, and humanity still sees the effects of one fateful decision.

What All Happened?

The results of the Fall led to catastrophic consequences. Alienation from God, sin, and death, the curse of original sin, and the ending of the earth's Edenic state. God was no longer physically accessible to walk through the Garden of Eden and commune with humanity. The Fall resulted in the human propensity to defy God's laws, a sinful nature. Adam was cursed to hard labour while Eve experienced pain in childbirth. Romans 8:20-22 describes how creation was subjected to frustration, groaning out of pain from the earth's fallen state.

Adam and Eve's Expulsion from the Garden. You Gotta Go.

Adam and Eve lost the privileges to their dream home, leaving the Garden of Eden, never to return. They would not continue to walk with God on this side of creation. They separated His physical presence, not able to see Him with their imperfect eyes.

The significance of a piece of fruit.

Is everything we suffer from the result of some juicy fruit two people ate? Doesn't seem fair to me.

To learn why the Fall led to such devastating consequences, one has to take the forbidden fruit into the context of Genesis, God, and His command. It was not any ordinary fruit. It was designated as a test of Adam and Eve's obedience to God, yet Adam and Eve trusted the serpent and ignored God. Everything was in a perfect state of joy, and they still wanted more than God had given them.

The consequences were so dire because God is both incredibly kind in his grace and severe in his reprimands. In His severity, He subjected Adam and Eve and creation to the effects of the Fall. Still, in His grace, He promised to be with and redeem them and their descendants. The forbidden fruit acts as a symbol of temptation everyone faces. God allows people to face the results of their good or bad decisions, but somehow, God can use evil and always turn it into good for those who love Him (Romans 8:28).

Why Is There So Much Evil? The Impact of Sin on Human Nature.

Everywhere one looks, everywhere one turns, evils and atrocities make one question the goodness of God. What is seen is not God's divine intervention but the result of sin and its impact on human nature. Sin caused a broken relationship with God, a fallen condition in the human heart, and alienation from others. According to Jeremiah 17:9, the heart "is deceitful above all things and beyond cure." Sin affected humanity's thoughts, desires, and actions, creating mistrust and strife amongst communities, leading to violence and all kinds of evil. Redemption from this nature can only be found in God.

What Does the Fall Teach Us? Its Theological Implications.

The first occurrence of the doctrine of original sin appears in Genesis; Adam and Eve pass down the inherent human propensity to sin to their descendants. Human depravity describes the gravity of man's sinful condition, that the human heart needs redemption and an atonement to reconcile them before God.

Allegory? Like Metaphors? Interpreting the Adam and Eve Story.

The literal and historical context of Genesis is a meaningful conversation, but can deeper, figurative meanings also be drawn from Genesis? Allegorical interpretations play a vital role in grasping lessons and values in Genesis. Adam and Eve, for example, can be seen as a representation of humanity; their relationship with God and their decision to sin reflects humanity as a whole and what they might have done in Adam and Eve's shoes.

One finds figurative elements in Genesis 1-3 that can act as allegories for overarching themes like moral choices, temptations, human nature's complexities, and the quest for knowledge. Allegories also promote interfaith dialogues, looking at themes and lessons found in biblical allegorical interpretations and comparing them to other religious texts.

Toil and Childbirth.

Adam and Eve faced severe consequences as a result of their disobedience. God curses Eve with pain in childbirth and a desire for her husband physically despite the pain. Adam is cursed to toil the ground with thorns and thistles, disrupting his efforts. He will soon farm by the sweat of his brow in the sweltering heat, dealing with the difficulties of weeds. God does not take sin lightly, as it is a direct rebellion to God's kingdom. Adam and Eve's story provides a valuable reminder that following down a sinful road will always lead to some form of physical, emotional, mental, or spiritual death.

Don't Look! God's Clothing of Adam and Eve.

God clothes Adam and Eve before they are sent out from the Garden, providing protection and showing His care for humanity, shielding them from vulnerability and shame. This act can symbolize a future atonement of Christ, clothing one's spiritual nakedness and shame.

Sounds Cool, Right? The Cherubim and Flaming Sword in Genesis 3:24.

Genesis 3:24 says, "After he drove the man out, he placed on the east side of the Garden of Eden cherubim and a flaming sword flashing back and forth to guard the way to the tree of life."

God placed an angel in front of the Garden of Eden so that Adam and Eve could not return in search of the fruit that made them live forever. God could not allow sinful humanity to live forever in their fallen state.

In Genesis 6, God decides to flood the earth because of how prevalent wickedness and violence is. This violence was in part due to the long lives humanity could live at the time, living up to 1,000 years old. God takes away this ability to live longer after the flood in the same way He took away immortality from Adam and Eve.

More and More People Every Year. The Growth of Human Civilization.

After being expelled from the garden, Eve gives birth to two boys, Cain and Abel, who are prominent in the Genesis narrative. In Genesis 4, the older brother, Cain becomes jealous of the younger brother because God accepts Abel's sacrifice more than Cain's. The sin of Cain's heart ultimately leads to his decision to kill Abel. Cain is afterward cursed and forced to wander the earth as a consequence of murder.

Genesis follows humanity's expansion and the familial lineages of Adam, documenting cultural aspects and historical events throughout its 50 chapters. As Adam's descendants spread throughout the earth, it's important to note urban centres formed with the development of job specializations in agriculture and shepherding.

Don't Wear it Out. The Biblical Meaning of Naming.

Naming in the Bible held deeper relational, cultural, and spiritual meaning than naming does in today's society. Back then, names carried significant weight to a person's future. In multiple instances, new names were given in Genesis and the New Testament. God renamed Abram to Abraham to become the "father of many nations." Names also reflected symbolism and prophecy. The major Old Testament prophets often had names related to their prophetic message from God.

Bible Basics

A Pretty Big Deal. Noah's Birth and Significance.

Noah exemplifies righteousness in a corrupt world and symbolizes hope and renewal. Noah represents the continuity of Adam's lineage as humanity progresses from the Garden of Eden to civilizations across the Ancient Near East. Noah's righteousness catches the attention of God's heart, deciding He will preserve humanity because of Noah's faithfulness.

Original Sin. It's Not a Good Thing.

Original sin describes how Adam and Eve's disobedience led to the subsequent sin nature all humans inherited. It led to moral corruption, a natural tendency to want to do the wrong thing in the eyes of God. This sinful nature is universal; everyone has a sinful nature before knowing Christ, God's Son.

Adam and Eve Get A Lot of Attention. Art and Literature.

Adam and Eve are widely referenced in literature and art, often as archetypes, appearing across periods and genres. One example is the literary retelling and adaptation of "Paradise Lost" (1667), written and adapted by John Milton. Adam and Eve are used in these works to symbolize the universal human experience, whether the complexities of human relationships, the struggle between good and evil, or a quest or curiosity for knowledge.

How Do They Compare? Creation Myths From Other Cultures and Genesis.

Creation accounts across cultures share central themes while varying on the specific details. Creation myths often describe chaos or nothingness, an initial state of the formless and void world. Creation myths and Genesis also describe the ordering of the cosmos into different stages. They typically describe how the cosmos and humanity are created from divine speech or the actions of a deity. The specifics differ, including the creator, the order of creation, and the origins and purpose of humanity.

A Man and a Woman. What Are Our Roles according to Genesis?

God created man and woman in His image, giving them equal worth before God and each other. God saw that man was alone and needed a suitable partner, creating a woman (Eve) to be one flesh with her husband (Adam).

Later in the Bible, it explains the roles of men and women in a marriage union. The Bible merely states the husband should love his wife like Christ loves the church, sacrificing himself daily for his wife. In the same way, a wife should submit to her husband's leadership (as long as he is not leading into her sin). Genesis 2:24 portrays marriage as a unity between a husband and wife, becoming "one flesh" physically, emotionally, and spiritually.

The Story of Adam and Eve Still Matters. Contemporary Discourse on Genesis.

Genesis is still relevant in cultural analysis, philosophy, psychology, gender studies, ethics, and theology. Adam and Eve's story contributes to discussions on the consequences of human actions, personal responsibility, the human condition, and the universal struggle against temptation. Genesis explores gender roles such as familial, partnership, and marriage relationships, leading to discussions on interpersonal, complementary, and equality within each. Genesis helps answer psychological and existential questions like: why are we here? What purpose do I serve? The beginning of Genesis also provides a starting point for interfaith and interdisciplinary dialogue, exploring the themes, reflections, and applications.

Theodicy. God Is Good in the Midst of Evil.

Theodicy: "the theological and philosophical approach that attempts to reconcile suffering and evil in the world with the belief that an all-knowing, all-powerful, benevolent God exists." Quite an academic task to achieve, but vital to a deeper understanding of God and a source of peace amid pain. Genesis is helpful to theodicy, pointing out the beginnings of evil, the role of moral responsibility, and how divine justice plays out.

Why Does Evil Exist in the World?

Why would God give Adam and Eve the option to disobey? Why not create a perfect world with no temptation? Free will and moral responsibility. Ultimately, God wants hearts that love him, not obligated to obedience.

Unfortunately, Adam and Eve chose to disobey, and humanity fell hard, leading to God's divine justice. God promised there would be difficulties in this life due to sin, but He promised to restore it one day, in this life (Romans 8:28) and the next (Revelations 21).

God promises to redeem and restore everything wrong on this side of earth. Suppose the suffering humanity experiences is compared with the eternity of perfection promised. In that case, it vastly outweighs the troubles of a comparatively short life. God is good, but sometimes it takes perspective, reflection, and, more often than not, time, to see that.

Conclusion.

God intended perfection for us but also wanted us to experience a personal relationship with Him. He could not force us to love Him.

Unfortunately, just like Adam and Eve, we fall. Hard. We've all walked away from God at some point and experienced the consequences of our decisions. However, that is not the end of the story. God walked through the Garden of Eden with Adam and Eve. One day, we too can walk with Him and experience a perfect, loving relationship.

You will experience trials and testing, but know it's not the end of the story. Death doesn't win. Sin doesn't win. God wins. And He will bring you home.

In the next chapter, we'll examine Cain and Abel and the dynamics that led to Cain's murder. God's justice wins in this story, cursing Cain for his grievous sin while showing mercy by promising to protect him as he wanders the earth alone. Justice and grace ultimately win in the end.

Chapter 3
Cain and Abel

"The story of Cain and Abel is the story of every person. It is not a story about two farms but about two lives. The question it poses is the same question that is addressed to each of us: 'If you do well, will you not be accepted?'"

— Wendell Berry

"Am I my brother's keeper?"

— Genesis 4:9b

If you've grown up with siblings, you know the tight bond and contentious relationship it can look like. As we read about Cain and Abel in Genesis 4, we find their relationship resembles anything but companionship.

Cain becomes jealous of God's favoured treatment of Abel. Eventually, the jealousy turns into a rage, ending with Cain murdering Abel. The story has severe implications on the

dangers of jealousy, God's requirement of justice, and the importance of owning one's feelings and actions.

Not a Good Idea Cain, The Consequences of His Actions.

In Genesis 4, Cain offers sacrifices to God that have less value
than his brother Abel's sacrifices. God looked favourably on
Abel's offering for providing the best of his flock, while not
regarding Cain's offering the same, providing produce as his
sacrifice. Cain envies Abel and God's favourable treatment of
him. (His parents likely favoured Abel as well).

Cain likely did not offer his best produce as a choice sacrifice,
demonstrating his lack of faith and appreciation for God's provision. At the end of the story, God curses Cain for murdering
Abel. Cain will be a wanderer for the rest of his life, away from
his family without a home to settle.

**What If I Admit I Was Wrong and Change? Sin and
Repentance.**

Reading the Old Testament, one might think God is pretty harsh.
To believe that God is good and loving, one must reconcile the
concepts of divine justice and grace.

In the story of Cain and Abel, we see Cain sins in his heart,
harbouring jealousy and anger towards Abel. God confronts
Cain's jealousy in Genesis 4:6-7, allowing him to repent and
change his attitude. Cain remains indignant, kills his brother, and
even denies taking responsibility for his thoughts and actions.

God curses Cain, giving him two opportunities to repent and
foster his own unique relationship with God. We find countless
stories of God in His justice punishing wickedness, yet willing to
turn back from it the moment His people admit their wrongdoing. God is a loving God, a God of justice who does not desire to
punish. However, He knows the human heart all too well. He

knows exactly what it needs and the depth of its evil if unchecked.

What We Can Learn From Cain and Abel.

Cain and Abel's story provides the first look at jealousy and envy and how destructive and dangerous it can be. Bitterness starts on a heart level with harbouring bad intentions, and if unchecked, it leads to more aggressive and violent ideation. Genesis 4 looks at the importance of responsibility and accountability. God confronts Cain on his feelings, still, Cain refuses to acknowledge the evil thoughts in his heart.

The consequences of sin are drastic, but righteousness and obedience will be blessed in the end. Cain and Abel teach the value of fraternal relationships and how complex familial relationships can be. Working through strong feelings towards family members or loved ones is important. If ignored or accepted, bitterness can consume a person's life, overshadowing all the good around them.

There's Something on Your Forehead. Interpretations of the Mark on Cain.

After God curses Cain, Cain despairs, saying he will be killed by anyone who sees and recognizes him. God promises to protect his life by putting "a mark" on Cain.

Just what exactly is the mark of Cain? Some believe that it was some kind of symbol of divine protection, that God would look over his life despite murdering his brother. It could have been a physical or a symbolic mark, such as a distinct physical trait or some form of stigma or social branding that people know was Cain, a marked man. Others believe the mark is more spiritually or metaphorically significant. It could be considered a mark of shame, a different state of consciousnesses, or a changed man.

Could They Still Talk One on One? Cain's Dialogue with God.

It's implied during Cain and God's dialogue that he still has a direct relationship with God and can communicate verbally or through conscious interaction. Cain's dialogue with God reveals the importance of human accountability, allowing Cain to admit his sin. God allowed Cain to own up to his feelings, but Cain hardened his heart instead. We see God's punishment and protection at work, balancing the importance of justice and showing mercy.

In Cold Blood. The Impact of Cain's Curse.

Cain's curse will affect the rest of his life. It entails agricultural consequences - the ground will no longer yield abundant crops, and his work will become more arduous. Cain will also be separated from his family, wandering the earth with no place to settle, living a life of isolation and loneliness. Cain likely experienced the social and psychological impact of feeling shame, guilt, and alienation from society. The curse reminds Cain of the spiritual and moral consequences of murder, separated from God's favour.

Let Us Build. The Development of Human Civilization After Cain.

The Bible does not provide a detailed account of the development of human civilization. Still, bits and pieces of information can show the progression. Genesis follows the lineage of Cain's descendants, mentioning his son Enoch and the building of a city, a new development in that period. It can be inferred that advancements and innovations, such as metallurgy, music, and livestock, occurred from Cain's descendants. We also find that human society progresses beyond nomadic lifestyles to incorporate specialized occupations in settled communities.

Bible Basics

As Close As Brothers. The Biblical Concept of Brotherhood.

Brotherhood in the biblical context implies a closeness experienced as siblings in a familial sense and closeness in a spiritual sense. In a literal sense, brotherhood refers to those who share the same lineage or parents, often associated with care, love, and support for each other.

The Bible also encourages us to treat each other in church as brothers or sisters, as the family of God. Jesus taught his followers kindness and compassion towards one another with mutual respect, solidarity, and empathy.

What About Other Characters? Sibling Dynamics in Biblical Stories.

Cain and Abel's sibling dynamics may be the first but not the last example. In Genesis 25-33, we find the dynamics between Jacob and Esau, how the older would serve the younger, and how they fought, only reconciling after years of separation. The story of Joseph and his brothers also portrays the role of jealousy and how rash decisions out of anger can affect relationships forever. The story of Joseph ends on a positive note. Joseph forgives his brothers and ends up saving their lives. David was treated with disregard by his older brothers but was then chosen by God to be the future king of Israel. God shows that He does not play favourites when it comes to His family. Every family member matters.

A Farmer and a Shepherd. The Significance of the Two Archetypes.

Cain's role as a farmer contrasts with Abel's role as a shepherd, more than just as an occupational difference. They have symbolic meanings, implying different devotions, faiths, and attitudes. Abel gave with a sincere heart out of worship, trusting God would provide if Abel gave him the best of his flock.

Conversely, Cain appears to give out of compulsion, not the best of his produce.

There is a spiritual significance between the two roles as well. Shepherding implies protection, care, and guidance, while farming represents patient cultivation, provision, and growth through the works of the hand. The farmer and shepherd archetypes represent different occupations, attitudes, and offerings, reflecting their heart conditions with God.

What Else Is There To Know About Cain's Story? The Broader Implications.

Cain's story reflects sin and its consequences, thoughts that can lead to decisions that result in lifelong repercussions. It shows the gravity of one's heart and the effects of one's choices. It emphasizes the importance of responsibility and accountability with a reconciliation mindset to start over and turn from a harmful, dangerous path.

It explores the dynamics of familial relationships how important it is to get one's relationships with family right, whether close or afar. Cain's story focuses on a person's worship and attitude towards God. We also see the continuity of the Genesis narrative, following Adam and Eve's descendants, later focusing on Noah and Abraham's descendants.

Who's to Say What is Just? God and Divine Judgment.

There are four significant occurrences of God's divine judgment in early Genesis. The judgment of Adam and Eve, Cain, the flood, and Babel.

God alone decides what is right and just and has the power to enforce His moral laws with severe consequences. God uses divine judgment as a deterrent so those who sin will reconsider their thoughts and actions and change after experiencing difficult consequences. Divine judgment is intended to be a wake-up call to remind people God is the divine judge.

What Was It Like Back Then? The Cultural and Historical Context.

During the time Cain lived, the human economy was dominated by nomadic societies as agricultural societies continued to develop. We see that Abel was a shepherd and Cain was a farmer, demonstrating the diversifying of specialized roles at the beginning of civilizations.

The offering of sacrifices was the Ancient Near Eastern tradition to appease or please the deities. Cain's murder of Abel reflects similar themes of fratricide found in ancient mythologies, often between siblings vying for power. During that time, oral tradition passed down a family's history and lineage. The story of Cain and Abel was likely taught and remembered from generation to generation through oral tradition before being written and recorded in the Bible.

There Was This Guy. Then There Was This Guy. Genealogies' Role in Genesis.

Genesis provides three lists of genealogies in Genesis 5, 10, and 11, following the generations of Adam to Noah, Noah's sons after the flood, and the descendants of Terah to Abraham.

These genealogies provided historical context for the periods between the central characters in Genesis, estimating when Noah and Abraham walked the earth. Providing genealogies highlights the continuity of and succession of previous characters, giving Genesis a direction, a connection between characters, and a chronological unfolding of events.

God promises Abraham's descendants will possess Canaan's land and follow his descendants throughout Genesis, Exodus, Leviticus, Numbers, Deuteronomy, and Joshua until they take Canaan as their own. Genealogies prove God's promises to Abraham and David and their future generations, promising descendants as numerous as the sands on the seashore and an heir to the throne.

Cain and Abel and Their Influence on Religious and Philosophical Thought

The story of Cain and Abel teaches the dangers of envy, how it can play a role in sibling relationships, and how to resolve jealousy at a heart level before it becomes deadly. Cain and Abel's story explores the importance of sacrificing and worshipping God with a sincere, generous heart rather than out of obligation.

What Does Cain Represent? Allegorical Interpretations.

Upon closer look, Cain and Abel as an allegory can represent good and evil. Cain represents evil demonstrated by selfishness, disobedience, and jealousy, while Abel represents good in his devotion to God, righteousness, and innocence.

Agriculture and pastoralism in Genesis 4 represent different values - agriculture symbolizes human growth, civilization, and societal development. In contrast, pastoralism is a more virtuous, simpler form of life in harmony with nature.

The envy Cain had in his heart can be interpreted as the inner spiritual struggles within each individual's heart. The power one's thoughts have on one's actions and the importance of assessing one's heart if it reflects envy, bitterness, or selfishness.

Did They Say That Already? The Role of Repetition in the Genesis Narrative.

Repetition is used throughout Genesis to reinforce key themes and elements within each story, highlighting the major takeaways from the narrative singularly and as a whole.

Repetition gives Genesis a rhythm and a flow that reads smoothly from story to story. The sections, phrases, and sayings repeated serve to clarify and amplify the most important message of that story. It was also typical for oral tradition and cultural transmission to use repetition to preserve each narrative's essential histories and teachings.

Repetition in Genesis creates an emotional effect, giving a sense of anticipation, emphasis, and urgency by heightening tension and conveying emotion.

Forgiveness and Reconciliation and Genesis 4.

Forgiveness and reconciliation are tricky subjects, and God is not afraid to address them. In Genesis 4, we find Cain being confronted by God to let go of his envy and bitterness towards Abel. God allows Cain to forgive, but Cain hardens his heart and kills his brother. Therefore, God must hold him accountable for the sake of His own justice but also for Cain's sake. Cain will experience suffering as his greatest teacher for his sin. He will learn the consequences that any sin he pursues will reap lasting, severe consequences. Cain will learn from his decision and reconcile with God if he softens his heart to God.

Cain's Legacy.

Cain is known primarily for his decision to murder. Still, other conclusions can be drawn from God's mercy, providing Cain with a mark of protection to live a longer life, not killed for his crime.

Cain's legacy also includes his and his descendants' contribution to city development, creating or improving upon certain skills that contributed to early civilizations. Cain's story serves as a deterrent to others contemplating sin to turn in the opposite direction, take account of the heart, and choose the right path, not facing the consequences that Cain did.

Sean Purcell

You're Not Invited. Cain's Exile and its Theological Implications.

Cain's exile reflects the gravity of sin and how it creates a separation between God and humanity. His exile also shows the role of moral accountability, that Cain would reflect on his decision for the rest of his life due to his exile. One way to interpret the severity of Cain's exile was so he would never do the same thing again. Cain's story may seem like only a curse, but God did show incredible mercy by not taking Cain's life. God, in His grace, promised a mark of protection. God still loves Cain, providing for him even after murdering his brother.

They Go Well Together. The Interconnectedness of Biblical Narratives.

There is an amazing interconnectedness throughout each book in the Bible, stories spanning over four millennia by 40 different authors, all inspired by God to write in their own unique styles across literary genres. Genesis displays a continuity of themes, including divine intervention, revelation, and justice. It provides genealogies and lineages related to later characters in the Bible. It foreshadows and fulfills prophecies, including the future development of covenantal relationships with Noah and Abraham.

Like Father. Like Son: Cain's Descendants and Their Significance.

In Genesis 4:17-24, the Bible mentions Cain's descendants: Enoch (Cain's first son), Irad, Mehujael, Methushael, and Lamech. Lamech is attributed to taking two wives, the first recorded account of polygamy in the Bible. He is known for his boastful attitude towards violence, killing two men for injuring/bruising him. Lamech's pride demonstrates the further moral degradation of Cain's lineage.

34

Conclusion.

Pretty intense, right? We've all been jealous before, but to kill your brother in cold blood? It's the first tragedy of the Bible. God gave Cain a chance, and Cain ignored it twice. He did not take accountability for his heart and his actions.

Has there ever been a time in your life when you were bitter towards someone? Maybe you were jealous of what they were, what they had, or what they did. That may apply to you still today. What parts of your heart have you ignored or left unexamined?

We've seen sin's harmful effects but will learn more about the beneficial effects of righteousness in the next chapter. The earth and humanity were preserved because of Noah's faithfulness. We, too, can experience the same recognition and blessings that Noah did.

Chapter 4
Noah and the Flood

"In Noah's Ark, we can see a symbol of the Church, for as the Ark saved the just from the flood, so the Church saves the just from the flood of sin."

— St Thomas Aquinas

"Make yourself an ark of gopher wood..."

— Genesis 6:14

At some point in your life, you may wonder: how can God exist in a world so evil? The atrocities committed throughout history seem to imply there is no benevolent God. He is powerless or too apathetic to change the world, if there is one.

However, in Genesis 6, we see that God does indeed pay attention to the affairs of man and plays an intimate role in our lives (collectively and individually). Evil was so pervasive in humanity then that "every inclination of the thoughts of the human heart was only evil all the time."

The world became so evil that God regretted creating humanity. However, one man caught his attention, seeing his good heart and good deeds. Noah, the only righteous man on earth then, became the conduit for preserving the rest of humanity.

He Must've Been a Good Guy. Noah's Righteous Character.

Genesis 6:9: "Noah was a righteous man, blameless among the people of his time, and he walked faithfully with God."

What stands out about Noah is not only his righteous character but the fact that his moral integrity and faithfulness persevered in a crooked and perverse generation. He was likely persecuted, badgered, and heckled by the people around him, not just for making the ark but for being a faithful follower of God. It takes resolve, trust, and resilience to remain faithful to one's principles, especially if persecuted daily for it. God favoured Noah because of his righteousness and blessed him for it.

That's A Lot of Animals. Building the Ark.

God was detailed in his instructions to build the Ark because He knew the devastation the Flood would cause, taking into account the number of animals Noah would have on the Ark. God instructed Noah to build the Ark out of gopher wood, a material historians cannot define precisely what type was used. Biblical experts say it could have been cypress, cedar, or an unknown or lost wood species. Although ambiguous, it could simply refer to the material quality used to protect Noah's family and the animals from the Flood.

Represent. The Symbolism of the Flood and the Ark.

The flood symbolizes the concept of divine judgment and how it can bring about renewal.

To give a great example, consider a just war - a conflict with loss of life that brings healing and restoration. When a benevolent nation defeats a belligerent, imperialist country, they stop the belligerent country from killing and subjugating other territories and groups of people. In the same way, God's judgment of his enemies can be seen as a pre-emptive effort to stop further evil, ultimately bringing about peace.

Why The Flood?

To erase widespread evil. Noah's generation was given plenty of opportunities to humble themselves before God. Instead, they laughed at God's warning, disdaining Him and Noah as His messenger. Throughout history, God reminds humanity of their place before God when they grow prideful.

That's Quite a Story. The Narrative Structure of the Flood Account.

Genesis 6-9 details these order of events: the introduction of Noah and his generation's wickedness (Genesis 6:1-4); God's decision to destroy the earth (Genesis 6:5-8); the building of the ark and gathering of the animals (Genesis 6:9-22); the entry into the ark (Genesis 7: 1-16); the flood (Genesis 7:17-24); the subsiding of the flood (Genesis 8:1-18); the exit from the ark and God's covenant (Genesis 8:20-22); God's covenant with Noah (Genesis 9:1-17); and the genealogy and conclusion of Noah and the flood account (Genesis 9:18-29).

Well Done, Noah. Lessons on Perseverance and Trust in God.

Noah's example of steadfastness is seen in his prioritization of God's commands over peer pressure. He faced ridicule from his peers building the ark, but he focused on God over their mockery. Noah believed God would do as He said, even something as unconventional as a worldwide flood.

It also took patience and perseverance to build an ark with such dimensions. Noah demonstrated trust in God's timing, waiting for the floodwaters to subside before exiting the ark.

What Do They Say? Comparative Flood Narratives From Other Cultures.

The Mesopotamians believed in a flood in the Epic of Gilgamesh - the story of Utnapishtim, a man who builds a boat that saves him, his family, and various animals from a flood sent by the gods to wipe out humanity and its corruption.

The Greeks believed in a similar myth of Deucalion and Pyrrha - two individuals who survived a worldwide deluge Zeus sent trying to erase humanity's wickedness.

The Hindus believed their god, Lord Vishnu, appeared to a hero, Manu, as a fish, warning Manu of a coming flood. Manu builds a large vessel ahead of time that preserves himself, sages, and an unspecified number of animals.

The Chinese believed in the myth of Yu the Great, recording how he stopped a massive flood, building channels and dykes to redirect the waters and save humanity from a great flood.

Why Did God Do That? The Ethical Implications of God's Judgment.

It seems harsh, right? To wipe out everyone besides one family?

One has to take into account the whole context of the situation before arriving at a conclusion. God demonstrates His justice throughout the Bible, but only after providing people, communities, and nations every opportunity to change directions and repent. God is merely holding them accountable for their actions. Humanity had hardened its heart to God. Nothing would convince them to obey God except for the consequences of their decisions.

Not only did Noah's generation face a fate of their own doing, but God decided to save humanity and give it a fresh start. This world is no longer as violent as in Genesis 6. God's judgment is a dichotomous of severity and restoration.

Why Mention That? The Narrative Purpose of the Ark's Dimensions.

The Bible mentions the ark's length, width, and height, proving the practicality of fitting everyone (Noah, his family, and the animals) on board and demonstrating the feasibility of the ark surviving the flood. It also reflects God's order and divine design. God is precise, deliberate, and intentional in what He does.

Noah needed meticulous planning to build as big a vessel as the ark. It emphasizes following God's instructions to every detail rather than just assuming what He wants. Noah chose obedience to God's direction over his own directives.

All of Them? The Role of Animals in the Flood Narrative.

Although the Flood wipes out the earth, God still decides to preserve the biodiversity of animals and ecosystems of the planet. (The flood likely caused a restructuring of the Earth's distribution of land, water, and the development of different topographies). He knows that humanity depends on them for survival.

Preserving animals for Noah's and future generations' sake demonstrates God's provision. No matter the circumstances, His people will always have enough to get through the circumstances He calls them to. It shows God's desire to restore life - animals once teeming on the earth - and provide food for humanity.

Are You Local or Global? The Global vs. Local Debate.

Surrounding the debate on the flood is the question of how big it was and how much devastation it caused.

Was it a global flood that covered the entire Earth? Was it limited to a particular region?

The literal interpretation is that a global flood covered everything on the earth - including the highest mountains - and killed every living thing outside the ark.

The local flood perspective believes the flood was a regional event, potentially as small as a river valley. Others propose the flood might have been regional, only large enough to kill humanity to the extent God decided.

What Changed? The Post-Flood World and Its Challenges.

Following the flood, humanity found an empty, desolate world that needed new societies and civilizations rebuilt. Noah and his descendants must re-establish society, culture, and governance.

The flood likely affected the earth's environment, ecosystems, weather patterns, and landscapes. Noah and his descendants also likely experienced agricultural challenges after the floodwaters removed agriculture and vegetation, making it difficult to initially regrow produce. They would need to preserve and take care of the animal kingdom until they reproduced and were plentiful to prevent extinction.

Divine Sorrow. The Concept of Divine Regret in the Flood Story.

In Genesis 6:5-7, the language of "regret" or "repentance" is anthropomorphic, attributing the human sentiment that God wishes something different had happened. It is a metaphorical way of communicating God's hurt and sorrow when He sees the evil hearts of men.

A Whole New World. The Connection Between The Flood and Creation.

Noah experiences a cleansing and renewal, a fresh start on the earth, similar to creation. As the world before creation was formless and void, the post-flood earth was bare and empty, allowing a fresh new start for humanity and creation.

We also see a reversal of creation. The land is covered by water in the flood account, and the opposite is in the creation account: the water is covered by land. In the same way God tells Adam and Eve to be fruitful and multiply, so Noah and his family are charged with repopulating the Earth.

God also establishes a covenant with Noah to preserve and care for his creation, just as He charges Adam and Eve.

Rebuild. The Impact of the Flood on Human Civilization.

Humanity began again from ground zero when Noah's descendants re-formed the civilizations that once populated the earth.

The flood caused cultural disruption and dispersal. Any recording would have been wiped out from the flood; only histories recorded through oral tradition would be remembered. Societal structures, infrastructure, and settlements needed to be rebuilt from scratch.

Could It Mean This? Allegorical Interpretations of the Flood Narrative.

The flood was used to wipe away all evil, giving the image that water's purifying and cleansing properties wash away the moral corruption and sin in the world.

The Flood gives insight into death and rebirth as well. For a seed to grow, it must die first to germinate from water, eventually growing into a thriving plant. In the same way, Romans 6:6 describes dying to oneself to put on a new life.

The flood can also represent the human psyche and the power of transformation. The floodwaters symbolize the human soul and mind in its chaos and turmoil; the ark symbolizes a place of sanctuary or refuge, providing growth and transformation opportunities.

We Need It. The Symbolic Meaning of Water in Biblical Literature.

In the New Testament, the importance of baptism and the use of water symbolizes new life, a before and after transformation being dipped in water.

Water is used throughout the Psalms and prophetic books to refer to God's presence, describing fountains, streams, and rivers as a refuge, a source of escape from the daily pressures of life.

Two Words. Environmental Stewardship. Lessons We Learn From the Flood.

The flood narrative teaches the values of caring for creation and preserving biodiversity, instructing every animal to enter the ark in pairs and safeguard their existence in nature.

It also shows the need to engage with nature in harmony and coexist with animals in their different environments. Once the animals left the ark, they likely migrated to the climates that suited them best. Noah, his family, and his descendants were also charged with preserving biodiversity by providing what the animals needed.

The conventional relationship God establishes through the image of the rainbow also applies to the animal kingdom. God promised not to erase life on earth by a flood again (including the animals).

Let's Make a Deal. God's Covenant With Noah and Its Theological Implications.

God made a covenant with Noah and his descendants, demonstrating His love for humanity despite the gravity of their evil towards Him and each other. God established this covenant with Noah and all generations following Noah, expressing the universal nature of His promise. He assures the continual existence of the earth, its sustenance of life, and the regularity of seasons, emphasizing His care for His creation.

Is It Significant in Other Parts of the Bible? The Flood in Later Books.

Psalmists and prophets sometimes metaphorize the flood, implying impending judgment or divine sin. The flood is also used to represent sin's consequences, water's purification, and divine judgment. The flood is a reminder of God's covenant, faithfulness, mercy, and judgment. Some view it as a precursor to baptism, the washing away of sin and the rebirth of someone's soul.

What Can We Learn From Noah? Noah as a Biblical Archetype.

In archetypal interpretation, Noah can be viewed as a survivor and a deliverer, God's conduit preserving humanity and animals. He is a covenantal figure, implying he is highly trustworthy and righteous before God (God's covenants rarely select men and women in the Bible).

Some view Noah as a foreshadowing of Christ. Why? In the same way that Jesus is a deliverer and source of salvation, Noah is a deliverer of humanity's continual existence, building the ark to protect himself, his family, and the animals.

Universal AND Particularistic Elements in the Flood Story.

Universal and particularistic elements? What?

Simply put, universal elements apply to humanity on a grand scale, and particularistic elements apply to particular individuals or cultures with specific details and narratives.

In the flood story, we find the universal elements of a global catastrophe, divine judgment, salvation and renewal, and God's covenant with creation. Particularistic elements include instructions given to Noah and his family for building the ark, the geographic and cultural context Noah lived in, and the ethical and moral lessons for that generation.

Conclusion.

So, what is the moral of Noah's story? Your heart and your good deeds don't go unnoticed. Evil towards you does not go unnoticed. Although you may be persecuted for your beliefs, God will right every wrong we face on this side of life. God sees you just like He saw Noah. Stay strong.

If you don't yet know God, I hope you learned from this chapter God is in the business of restoring. He started over with Noah and can do the same with you.

Although the dichotomy between divine justice and grace seems at odds, God sees each situation from the past, present, and future from every angle to make the most just and wise decisions. He corrects and punishes evil for the sake of His people. He disciplines those He loves, not out of anger but out of His desire to mature, strengthen, and grow us into more loving, joyful, and peaceful individuals.

You likely noticed the central role that water plays in the story of Noah. It symbolizes the purification that God performs on hearts like yours and mine. God is in the business of wiping the dust, the stains, the gunk off your heart and bringing it back to life, forgiving and restoring.

In the next chapter, we'll discuss pride's role in our relationships and how it affected Noah's descendants, attempting to build a monument to heaven. Pride got the best of them, and God chose to bring them back down to earth, reminding them of their place in the world. Humility reminds us God is at the centre of the universe. When no longer so important, we experience the freedom and peace of a God-centred life.

Chapter 5
Tower of Babel

"By the confusion of tongues, the Lord defeated the wicked counsel of the men who built the tower, and by a miracle declared that they were unworthy to build it."

— John Calvin

"Come, let us go down and confuse their language..."

— Genesis 11:7

In Genesis 11, humanity bands together to create a tower to reach the heavens. They unite to build a massive city and a monument that they can worship as the fruit of their efforts. God immediately recognizes the danger of pride in their hearts and disperses humanity. Why? So that they will not become so prideful and self-sufficient that they forget and disdain God. God intervenes on behalf of humanity as He did in Noah's generation, preventing worldwide corruption.

What We Want and What God Wants. Human Ambition and Divine Intervention.

Human ambition is "an earnest desire for some type of achievement or distinction" or "to seek after earnestly."

In the story of the tower of Babel, one reads about humanity's ambition to glorify themselves. In response to humanity's pride and efforts, God causes confusion amongst the builders, supernaturally introducing different languages. Suddenly, people speak different languages that only some around them can understand. There's no way to build the tower in this state of chaos because they cannot guide and instruct one another on what to do. They are forced to band together in separate groups of the same language and migrate to an uncharted land.

Pride Comes Before the Fall. Lessons on Pride and Humility.

The Bible mentions "humility" and "humble" throughout the Old and New Testaments, often used to describe a person repenting their sins and asking for forgiveness. James 4:6 mentions that God listens to the prayers of a repentant heart but does not bend to the prayers of the proud.

God often reminds humanity of their place in the world, created beings with little control of their lives that He can give and take away.

You're In Trouble. Linguistic Diversity as a Consequence.

Although the Bible is unclear about how many languages appeared in Genesis 11, it was likely a significant number. The Bible records all of civilization was centred at the site of Babel, building a great city and tower to the heavens. If God had only introduced a couple languages, the people still had an excellent chance to continue building. If hundreds of languages were given, building the tower would be impossible. At that point, they would have to disperse, forming groups with the same linguistics and establishing their own society and culture. Today's estimated number of languages is 7139, so God had to have introduced a significant number.

It Still Matters. The relevance of the Tower of Babel in Modern Times.

Today's unity and diversity in a globalized world results from the Tower of Babel - people speaking different languages. They were each given by God for others to communicate and understand, reflecting God's creativity.

God can speak every language He's created with people from all different backgrounds, cultures, and dialects. One learns in Revelations that heaven will consist of "a great multitude that no one could count, from every nation, tribe, people, and language."

Nimrod. It's A Name. His Role in the Biblical Narrative.

Nimrod, mentioned briefly in Genesis 10:8-12, is known as an expert hunter and prominent descendant of Ham, Noah's son. He is recorded in the Bible building several cities in the Mesopotamian region, including Calneh, Accad, Erech, and, most importantly, Babel. Nimrod is often associated with the development of urbanization and early civilization. Although little is known about him, biblical scholars believe he was likely a tyrant and arrogant towards God, inferred by his involvement in constructing the tower of Babel. His focus was on human achievement rather than divine authority.

United for All the Wrong Reasons. The Significance of a United Humanity.

God recognized united humanity would be able to achieve anything they put their mind to, growing prideful of what their hands made. Their ability to construct and innovate towards a shared objective would lead to direct conflict between God and humanity. The Tower of Babel demonstrates how easy it is to fall for pride.

Goodbye. The Dispersion of People and the Formation of Nations.

When linguistic confusion occurred, it dispersed people throughout the Earth, forming nations and cultures with different ethnic, cultural, and linguistic groups. God not only created their languages but was and is intimately involved in their development and history - every nation, region, and culture.

When, Where, and Why. The Context of the Tower of Babel.

The Tower of Babel existed within Mesopotamia in the Ancient Near East, sharing motifs and narratives similar to those of the Babylonian and Sumerian civilizations. The Babylonians and Sumerians embarked on large construction projects like the Tower of Babel, believed in divine intervention, and recorded the dispersal of humanity. The Mesopotamians built ziggurats, religious temples, and other symbols of political and cultural ambition, urbanizing into more prominent civilizations during this period.

He Always Wins. Lessons on Human Cooperation and Divine Sovereignty.

No matter how much humanity wanted to glorify themselves through the Tower of Babel, they were reminded they were at the mercy of an all-powerful God.

The concept of free will and divine sovereignty plays a significant role in the Tower of Babel as well as the story of Jonah.

If you don't know the story of Jonah, Jonah was called by God to prophesy to the Israelites' enemies, the Assyrians, specifically the Ninevites. Jonah tried to run away in the opposite direction, yet his escape was short-lived. Long story short, he ended up being thrown overboard a ship during a perilous storm. He was eaten in the belly of a large fish and transported to Nineveh after spending 3 days in the belly of the fish. God was determined to use Jonah.

Jonah resisted God's calling, but God did not take no for an answer. He acted in His divine sovereignty to use Jonah. Could Jonah have continued to resist God's calling? Yes, technically. It would have likely ended in the same result, though.

God has the sovereign power to do as He pleases in the lives of humanity. Still, He never forces anyone to choose Him. He leaves that a personal decision.

The Ancient Near East and Their View of the Tower of Babel.

The Tower of Babel resembles Mesopotamian texts, describing temple construction and ziggurats, which are stepped pyramid-like structures. They were often used in ancient religious practices to connect heaven and earth, a direct access to the spiritual, mythological, and eternal world. Mesopotamian texts describe how the gods divinely intervened when they witnessed the building of a large tower, similar to the biblical narrative of Babel. Mesopotamian myths also mention the gods introduced languages to confuse and scatter the people.

Judaism and Islam. The Tower of Babel in Rabbinic and Islamic Traditions.

While sharing similar narratives, Rabbinic and Islamic traditions incorporate additional teachings, interpretations, and details about the Tower of Babel. Rabbinic traditions include Midrashic literature and explanations that focus more on the ethical and moral lessons of the Tower of the Babel rather than the actions and motivations of humanity at the time. They highlight the importance of God's punishment for arrogance and teach lessons on unity and communication.

Islamic traditions have a similar story in Surah Al-Ma'daih (5:28-31). They interpret God's intervention at the Tower of Babel as a divine response to humanity's defiance of His laws. They focus on humility before divine authority and obedience to God's commands.

What Can We Interpret from Tower of Babel? An Allegory.

The tower's construction symbolizes excessive pride and man's attempt to challenge God's divine authority. The lack of humility in the story resulted in disunity and chaos, demonstrating pride's grievous effects. The Tower of Babel also reflects the importance of communication and understanding, how it unified humanity as one civilization, and how powerful it can be for ill or good. The tower is a metaphor for the spiritual ascent, humanity's efforts to reach transcendence, or spiritual enlightenment.

Art and Literature and the Tower of Babel's Role.

The Tower of Babel has been depicted by artists in paintings and illustrations (such as Pieter Bruegel the Elder, Gustave Dore, and Lucas Van Valckenborch), sculptures and reliefs (in public spaces, cathedrals, and churches), and architectural references (through spires, ziggurat-like structures, and towers).

Writers have portrayed the Tower of Babel in poetry and epic works (exploring themes like the consequences of pride, divine intervention, and human ambition), novels and short stories (exploring allegories through contemporary settings), and dramatic interpretations (exploring the human condition).

The Tower of Babel's Impact on the Development of Linguistics.

God's divine intervention at Babel caused the diversity of languages humanity has today.

It is important to note that humans all spoke the same language from Creation until the Dispersion, passed down from generation to generation. Developing hundreds of languages would only be possible if there was divine intervention. Entire new languages, let alone hundreds would take millennia or even mega years to create. New languages take time to separate the old from the new, introducing new words and forgetting words previously used. Other languages had no context unless a supernatural event or effect occurred. In this case, it was God's introduction of languages and the dispersal of humanity.

What Did We Learn? The Limits of Human Ambition.

Humanity decided to do what was right in their own eyes, and God demonstrated their eyes deceived them. They thought they would be great by worshipping themselves and their accomplishments. At any point, if human ambition becomes about self-reliance apart from God, it is rejection of God's role as Creator and Sustainer. Eager ambition must partner with humility, trust, and direction. A good plan might get in the way of God's great plans.

What Culture(s) Do You Associate With? Its Origins and the Tower of Babel.

The Tower of Babel led to distinct languages, bringing about new cultures, ethnicities, and traditions that changed over time, depending on the topography and locations they migrated towards and their interactions and infusions from other cultures. Diverse languages and cultures not only resulted from the Tower of Babel but developed from historical developments, environmental influences, migration patterns, and potential geographic isolation. Empirical data and multidisciplinary research complement Genesis' account of language diversity and its origins.

God Can and Does Intervene In Human Affairs.

God is incredibly involved in His creation, and humanity cannot see God at work. The Bible highlights the specific ways God intervenes in human affairs.

God constantly intervenes in human affairs, but one cannot understand what God is precisely up to at every moment. It is above anyone's pay grade. It is not man's role to demonstrate and predict the specifics of God's actions.

The Tower of Babel is one demonstration of God's authority, intervening when human ambition crosses the line. Throughout the Old Testament, God acts as people and nations obey/disobey Him. God punishes evildoers out of a desire to protect the poor, the marginalized, and the vulnerable. He rewards the righteous because of their faith. He does as He pleases in accordance with His nature and divine purpose.

A Warning Story. Stop. The Tower of Babel.

Numerous cautionary tales are found in the Bible, whether the Israelites' constant rebellion in the Old Testament or Annas and Saphira in the New Testament. God uses these cautionary tales to warn what others will experience if they choose evil over God. At Babel, humanity is forced to separate because they directly rejected God in their self-glorifying efforts to build a tower to reach the heavens.

What Do The Experts Say? Contemporary Religious Dialogue.

Clergy and religious experts continue to analyse Genesis 11's themes of humility and divine authority and how human ambition can be overridden by a higher power such as the God of the Bible. The story also provides a look at ethical reflection, to consider one's thoughts, ways, and actions and turn back from any path detrimental to oneself or their relationship with God. The Tower of Babel is useful for interfaith dialogue, contributing to conversations on humility, values, and the limitations of humanity before God. Discussions about religious, cultural and linguistic differences and their importance can be interpreted through the Tower of Babel.

Where Are We Going? The Biblical Theme of Scattering.

God's divine intervention of scattering humanity and his followers occurs at least four times in the Bible. In Adam and Eve's story, God's intention for humanity is to multiply and scatter to discover the ends of the Earth. In the dispersion following the Flood, God charges Noah to continue the lineage of Adam and Eve and repopulate the Earth. Scattering occurs later in the Old Testament when the Israelites rebel against God, leading to their exile within Babylon in the 6th century BCE. In the last scattering, Jesus calls his disciples and future believers to go to the ends of the Earth, spreading the Gospel in His Great Commission.

Pride and the Tower of Babel.

Humanity decided to build the tower to glorify their ingenuity and achievement. They wanted to unite, claiming their own authority over the world. God intervened, reminding humanity of its place and their need for God to provide, care for, and sustain their lives.

Conclusion.

So, what's the lesson to learn from the Tower of Babel?

You might think, *It's not like I have any strong desire to build a tower in my backyard, defy city permits, and reach the heavens!*

It may seem absurd in today's context, but what about other sources of pride in our modern world? What makes us prideful? Money? Our talents? Education? Appearance? Our social status? So many aspects of our lives can and often do make us prideful (or insecure). Pride can take over if we are not careful to reflect on our view towards ourselves, others, and God.

Why is pride so dangerous? Pride states to God or others, whether you realize it or not, "I'm better than you. I don't need you. I'm more than you." It may sound like you don't have this in your life. However, it can be much subtler than we think.

Consider what you're good at. Think about who you are. Do you ever think: "I'm better than them!" Or do you feel insecure, wishing you had some character trait or quality somebody else has?

If yes, consider Genesis 11 and reflect on what makes you feel prideful or insecure. The cure to pride and insecurity is humility, a modest evaluation of your worth. Humility does not degrade and does not inflate. Take some time to reflect on this.

The next chapter will focus on Abraham, the father of faith, and how his trust in God was greatly rewarded for him and future generations.

Chapter 6

Abraham

"In the history of Abraham, the Lord would teach every soul the great lesson that we must trust His promises however dark our prospects, and believe that He is our friend, and will never disappoint the faith that is reposed in Him."

— Ellen G. White

"Go from your country, your people, and your father's household to the land I will show you."

— Genesis 12:1

Abraham is an honoured hero of faith, leaving his family and country behind and trusting that God would provide for him. He believed God would make him the father of many nations, with descendants as numerous as sands on the seashore. It might be easy to read the story, gloss over the details, and think to yourself,

It must not be that hard to put ALL your hopes, dreams, and future into God's hands like Abraham did.

If you have any experience making a dramatic change in your life - whether moving to a new city for college or a job - you know just how scary it can be. The unknowns and what-ifs. Abraham gave up EVERYTHING, even willing to sacrifice his beloved son. That took extraordinary faith.

Was it impossible? No. Was it terrifying, putting his life in the hands of God? Absolutely. Faith means facing the unknown and believing God will take care of you all along the way.

To Where Now? Abraham's Journey of Faith.

Abraham lived in Ur until 75 years old. In his older age, God called Abraham to move from his hometown to the land of Canaan, the destination God promised his descendants would live. As the bird flies, the trek from Ur to Canaan is around 600-700 miles, but Abraham stops along the way as God guides him. The distance was no small feat for a man his age travelling with his family, including his wife Sarah, his nephew Lot, and their households.

I Promise To…The Covenant with Abraham.

God established a covenant with Abraham, promising Abraham would have descendants as numerous as the stars in the sky and an everlasting home in Canaan's fertile, diverse land.

God performs a sacrificial ceremony in Genesis 15 to solidify His covenant with Abraham for eternity. God begins the ceremony by having Abraham prepare an animal on an altar. He then puts Abraham in a deep sleep and appears in physical form during Abraham's slumber, walking between the divided animal pieces Abraham prepared at the altar. God passing in between the prepared sacrifice symbolizes the covenant's permanence.

(Abraham is fast asleep during the sacrificial ceremony because he cannot witness God with his eyes; God is too glorious for man's imperfection).

God also institutes circumcision as a sign of the covenant, a reminder to Abraham and his future descendants of God's setting apart of Abraham's descendants and their divine purpose.

After making a covenant with God, Abram's name changes to Abraham, reflecting his new role as "the father of many nations."

God Will Provide The Sacrifice. Mount Moriah and Isaac as a Test of Faith.

In Genesis 22, a tense situation occurs. God commands Abraham to sacrifice his beloved son, Isaac, as a burnt offering to God. Understandably, Abraham must have been conflicted, knowing God would provide descendants as numerous as the sands on the seashore through his lineage. At the same time, He was asking Abraham to kill Isaac, his promised heir.

Regardless of what he is feeling, Abraham does as he is told, journeying to Mount Moriah, where God wants Abraham to sacrifice Isaac. While traveling, Isaac asks which lamb will be sacrificed, not knowing God's command and his father's intentions.

How does Abraham respond? God will provide the offering.

The Bible does not explain exactly how it happened. Abraham likely bound Isaac to the altar with little warning, not until the time came to prepare the sacrifice. After binding Isaac to the altar, Abraham lifts his knife to sacrifice Isaac to God. As Abraham prepares to kill Isaac, an angel of the Lord suddenly appears and stops Abraham's hand.

Abraham passed the test. Was he willing to sacrifice everything for the sake of God, even his own son?

Yes.

After testing Abraham's faith, God divinely intervenes, providing a ram caught in a thicket to replace Isaac as the offering.

At This Moment in History. The Historical Context of Abraham's Life.

The Bible introduces Abraham as a wealthy man from Ur, the ancient Mesopotamian city in present-day southern Iraq. It was known then for its distinctive religious practices, diverse culture, and advanced civilization. Sumerians significantly influenced the region, introducing achievements in agriculture, architecture, and writing (cuneiform script).

Abraham is constantly on the move in Genesis, a nomadic figure searching for new pastures for his flock. Abraham lived during the Bronze Age, when tools and weapons of copper and tin expanded the efficiency of agriculture, leading to the rise of Mesopotamian city-states. Trade routes also facilitated cultural diffusion and assimilation with surrounding civilizations.

The High Order of Melchizedek. Abraham's Encounter.

In Genesis 14:17-24, Abraham encounters a man, Melchizedek, Salem's renowned king and priest. An influential figure with eternal significance, Melchizedek's name translates as "King of Peace" or "King of Righteousness."

Abraham encounters Melchizedek after rescuing his nephew Lot from captivity. Upon their encounter, Melchizedek graciously provides bread and wine and speaks a blessing over Abraham and his descendants. Abraham then offered a tenth of his spoils from his military campaign, later introducing the concept of tithing in the Bible.

The fact that Melchizedek blessed Abraham and received a tithe from Abraham demonstrates that Melchizedek had superior authority. Melchizedek holds symbolic and theological significance, portrayed as both a king and a priest just as Jesus is presented in the New Testament.

Location. Location. Location. The Significance of God's Promise to Abraham.

God promised Canaan to Abraham as his future inheritance, giving him and his descendants the best the world has to offer. Canaan is a prosperous land at the centre of the most influential civilizations. Later to be named Israel, Canaan became a part of the Israelites' identity, a land God forever promised to be theirs.

Circumcision and Its Theological Implications.

Circumcision was instituted to identify that Abraham and his descendants are God's chosen people, a visible mark they are set apart from the nations around them. Circumcision was viewed as a rite of passage for the Israelites, essential for males on the eighth day after birth.

In the New Testament, Paul teaches that setting apart a Christian's heart for God is a sign of spiritual circumcision, carrying significance in the New Covenant between God and humanity.

Praying For Them? Abraham's Intercession for Sodom and Gomorrah.

Abraham appeals to God for the wicked cities of Sodom and Gomorrah, to relent and not punish them. Abraham prays that if God finds a certain number of righteous men and women in the two cities, to spare Sodom and Gomorrah. Abraham starts with the number of fifty righteous individuals, continuing to intercede until he arrives at ten. God promises if ten righteous men or women are found in Sodom and Gomorrah, He will not wipe them out. The power of intercessory prayer is directly displayed in Abraham's encounter with God.

Hospitality Was Different Back Then. Lessons From Abraham's Example.

Abraham welcomes three visitors who arrive at his doorstep, serving these strangers with food, refreshments, and rest immediately after arrival. Abraham provides such hospitality to people he's never met, displaying an attitude of humility rather than allowing pride to guide his demeanour. How do the guests reward Abraham's hospitality? With God's promise that Abraham and Sarah would have a son named Isaac.

Match Up. How Do Abraham and Sarah Compare to Others?

Abraham and Sarah's treks (from Ur to Canaan to Egypt and back to Canaan) relate comparatively to other patriarchal figures (like Isaac and Rebekah and Jacob and Rachel) who experienced challenges and trials together. Their narratives portray the complexities and fragilities of family relationships. Each of these families experience conflicts in the household, infertility, and sibling rivalries, for example.

What separates Abraham and Sarah from the other characters in Genesis is their overwhelming generosity to the three unexpected visitors. The depth of Abraham and Sarah's faith also set them apart, providing them a well of blessings through an eternal covenant. They experienced incredible trials and grew in patience together. Sarah's barrenness was difficult for them both. Even when there was no human possibility of pregnancy, God fulfilled His promise.

The Wanderer and Sojourner. Abraham. The Man, The Myth, The Legend.

Abraham's wandering represented his divine calling and obedience, constantly tested to rely on God's provision. Abraham was often a stranger in foreign lands. His legacy demonstrates that God calls His followers to rely constantly on Him to deepen their faith.

You Promise? The Significance of the Covenant God Made With Abraham.

The Old Testament describes the Israelites as God's chosen people, meant to be a light and a reflection of God worldwide. God promises Abraham and his descendants divine favour, protection, and blessings with an everlasting and unconditional covenant. God will always be with His people, even amidst his divine justice.

Cool Name. The Significance of the Name, Isaac.

Isaac means "he laughs," or "laughter," referring to Sarah's laughter at the mention she would bear a child in her old age. Sarah's disbelief in the prophecy turns into joy when she gives birth to Isaac. Isaac's name reminds Abraham and Sarah that God is faithful to His promises, no matter how far-fetched the promises seem.

What Happened There? Abimelech and Abraham.

On his way to Gerar, Abraham encounters King Abimelech. Abraham was afraid Abimelech or his people would kill Abraham when they saw how beautiful Sarah was, deciding to lie to Abimelech that Sarah is his sister. Abimelech notices Sarah's beauty and decides he wants to take her as his wife. Despite Abraham's decision to lie, God protects both Abraham and Sarah, appearing to Abimelech in a dream and warning him to return Sarah to Abraham unharmed or face death for taking Abraham's wife.

Abimelech immediately returns Sarah, rebuking Abraham for presenting Sarah as his sister. Abimelech however provides restitution, giving Abraham livestock and a choice of land in the region. Even though Abraham took matters into his own hands to protect himself and Sarah, God watched over and protected them.

Human Intervention. The Hagar and Ishmael Narrative.

Before becoming pregnant with Isaac, Sarah believed she would not be able to give Abraham a child in her barrenness and old age. She took matters into her own hands, presenting her maidservant Hagar as a surrogate mother to have a child for her. Abraham complies with her request, and Hagar gives birth to Abraham's first child, Ishmael. However, tensions arise within the household as Sarah begins to mistreat Hagar. She grows jealous after Hagar gives birth to Ishmael and becomes even more combative when she gives birth to Isaac.

Hagar ultimately decides to run away with Ishmael because Sarah's treatment of them is so severe. Hagar becomes lost in the desert, on the brink of despair and death. When hope seems lost for Hagar, God intervenes by providing Hagar and Ishmael with water and a promise that Ishmael will be the father of a great nation.

The Expulsion of Hagar and Ishmael and Its Significance.

The family conflict between Hagar and Ishmael and Sarah and Isaac reaches its breaking point when Sarah sees Ishmael mocking Isaac. Sarah demands Abraham cast out Hagar and Ishmael. Abraham feels caught up in the dilemma with a difficult choice to make.

God assures Abraham that he will bless Ishmael and make a great nation out of his descendants. God directs Abraham to send Hagar and Ishmael away to the wilderness of Beersheba, giving them bread and water for their journey.

Hagar and Ishmael's expulsion shows the division in Abraham's family line. The Ishmaelites would later form the Arab nations and tribes surrounding Israel to this day. (They've engaged in constant conflict dating back to the family conflict between Sarah, Hagar, Isaac, and Ishmael).

Quite the Negotiator. Abraham's Discussion With God Over Sodom.

God divinely revealed to Abraham through His three guests that He would investigate the cities of Sodom and Gomorrah to see if the outcry of their wickedness was true. God will destroy the cities if their unrighteousness is as evil as He has heard.

Abraham pleads for the two cities out of deep concern for the righteous and their well-being. He prays for God to spare the cities if He can find 50 righteous men, then 45, then 40 until he arrives at the number 10. If 10 righteous people are found, God promises to relent from His punishment.

This discussion between God and Abraham has profound implications for humanity's human-transcendent relationship with God, able to intercede on behalf of each other.

Got Me All Bound Up. The Binding of Isaac. Its Symbolism and Implications.

Genesis 22: 1-19 is rich with symbolism, foreshadowing Christ's death on the cross. In the same way that Isaac carried the wood for his own sacrifice, Jesus carried the cross to Calvary as a voluntary sacrifice to be crucified.

Isaac did not fight Abraham as he bound and placed him on the altar. He submitted to his father's will. Jesus reflects the same submission and willingness to die for His Father, obedient to death on the cross.

The binding of Isaac shows the faith and obedience of both Abraham and Isaac. It was a test of their loyalty. Did they love God more than life itself and their love for one another?

I Want To Be Like Him. Abraham, the Model of Faith in the New Testament.

Abraham is mentioned extensively as a model of faith in Romans 4:1-25 and Hebrews 11:8-19 in the "Hall of Faith" passage. Paul describes that Abraham's faith was credited to him as right-eousness because he believed God would fulfil His promises, giving Abraham a son through his wife Sarah (even in her old age and barrenness). In the Hall of Faith, the author honours Abraham for trusting God enough to leave his home country in search of the foreign land of Canaan. Hebrews mentions Abraham believed God could resurrect Isaac from the dead if he sacrificed Isaac to God.

Abraham Is Pretty Important, Even in Islam.

Abraham, known as "Ibrahim" in Arabic, is a central figure of the prophets of Islam. He is venerated for his submission, obedi-ence, and faith in God's will. His teachings and story can be found in various Surahs (chapters) in the Qur'an. Ibrahim, in Islamic tradition, is known for monotheism and iconoclasm, preaching against the polytheism and idol worship of his genera-tion, declaring that there was One God, Allah, and all other worship is idolatrous.

Ibrahim is attributed to building the Kaaba (found in Mecca) with his son Ishmael, or "Isma'il." The Qur'an states that Allah commanded them to build a place of worship, a sacred house for a holy pilgrimage. Islamic tradition believes Ibrahim prepared to offer Isma'il as a sacrifice (rather than Isaac), displaying Ibrahim's faith and obedience to God.

The Best Teacher? Testing. Lessons from Abraham.

Abraham was unwavering in trusting God, even when it went against human reasoning. He immediately obeyed God's commands, leaving his homeland as soon as God revealed himself, circumcising himself and his household at God's command, and tying Isaac to the altar willingly, ready to sacrifice his son.

Abraham persevered in the waiting, trusting God would still provide a son. He showed concern for others, praying for the righteous living in Sodom and Gomorrah. His faith was tested, displaying it when he needed it most.

Abraham's Story and Ethical Thought.

Abraham faced a profound ethical dilemma when God asked him to sacrifice his son Isaac. Abraham felt conflicted, questioning his personal morality of killing another human being, let alone his son, as a sacrifice to God. He had to decide between obeying a divine command or trying to save his son's life.

Abraham exemplified selflessness to trust God's plans over his own. God's promise to Abraham and Sarah was irrational; no woman at Sarah's age, especially a barren woman, could become pregnant and give birth. It made no rational sense, but Abraham chose faith over his own ability to rationalize.

Conclusion.

Following God is easy when circumstances go well, and we are not asked to do anything remotely out of our comfort zone. The honeymoon stage of relationships, including with God, does not last forever. There will be tests and trials, just as God promised.

At some point in your walk, you will be tempted to doubt God, question God, berate God, and point out the injustice of it all. God disciplines the children He loves. Our faith is tested the most during those times. Faith is the only thing left after the fire has refined us.

When you experience trials, remember examples like Abraham, a man of willing and immediate obedience. Faith means trusting in God's direction, even when we can't see past the clouds. Even when we cannot rationalize when we get out of the trials we face, trust that God has a plan in all of it and that if we hold steadfast and remain faithful, it will come to fruition.

In Chapter 7, we will look at the relationship between Sarah and Hagar and the complexities of family relationships. Sarah took matters into her own hands, causing conflict and division within the family. As hard as it is to wait, God's plans are always better than ours.

Chapter 7
Sarah and Hagar

"The story of Sarah and Hagar challenges us to confront the intersections of race, class, and gender. It prompts us to consider the ways in which power dynamics shape relationships and influence the treatment of individuals."

— Nyasha Junior

"The Lord has kept me from having children. Go, sleep with my slave; perhaps I can build a family through her."

— Genesis 16:2

We previously discussed Abraham's faith, but now let's look at the dynamics of Abraham's household between his wife Sarah and maidservant Hagar. Sarah believed she could not bear Abraham any children in her old age so she requested Abraham sleep with her Egyptian slave, Hagar, so that Sarah could claim Abraham's family line using Hagar as a surrogate mother.

After conceiving a child, Hagar grows prideful and disdains Sarah; Sarah displays harsh treatment in return. It becomes so severe that Hagar decides to run away. However, God intervenes, speaking to Hagar to return to Sarah, promising Hagar will have numerous descendants through her child. Hagar gives birth to Ishmael, and a family conflict erupts later. Sarah witnesses Ishmael mocking Isaac in Genesis, jealous and enraged, demanding that Abraham cast them out again.

As Hagar wanders the desert of Beersheba, she gives up, losing hope that she or Ishmael will survive the desert, and die of dehydration. God reassures Hagar, divinely revealing her descendants will form great nations and then provides her water to continue her journey.

What can we learn from this whole story? Wait. Wait on God's timing. It's difficult. It feels like forever.

Why wait? Because God's plans are always better than anything we can dream of. Had Sarah waited on God's promise, the conflict and tension she experienced would've been avoided.

Sarah and Hagar's relationship is a good look at complex familial relationships, teaching valuable lessons on navigating those dynamics and what not to do.

Still Abraham's Descendant. The Birth of Ishmael.

Although Ishmael was born outside God's covenant to provide an heir, his birth holds significance. Ishmael would later father twelve sons with a lineage of tribes that strongly impacted the Middle East. Biblical scholars believe the Ishmaelites would later make up much of the Arabs' Middle Eastern history and culture. Islam believes Ishmael built the Kaaba in Mecca with his father, Ibrahim.

Just Wait. Patience and Trust in God's Timing.

Sarah and Abraham waited years for God to fulfil His promise, experiencing their bodies age, likely not feeling the strength and vitality they once had to raise a child.

Still, they waited.

Eventually, in a time of weakness, Sarah lost some of her faith, deciding to force the issue of providing a descendant. She gave her maidservant, Hagar, to Abraham as a concubine to bear a child.

This inevitably led to conflicts that would not have occurred had she waited. What does this teach? Avoid hasty decisions while waiting and trust God will come through in His timing.

What Can We Learn from Sarah and Hagar?

The story of Sarah and Hagar demonstrates God's ability to redeem any decision and turn it into good, even amid imperfections. Despite the mess Sarah made, God still provided for Hagar and Ishmael while He promised Abraham and Sarah that they would still have their own son.

Hagar's Meeting With the Lord's Angel.

After being treated harshly by Sarah, Hagar runs away for the first time, trying to find a place where she can raise Ishmael without Sarah's mistreatment. Hagar arrives at a spring in the wilderness where an angel of the Lord appears, telling her to "go back to your mistress and submit to her," promising to increase her descendants "so much that they will be too numerous to count."

This encounter demonstrates God's concern for Hagar and those facing distressing circumstances. He has a heart for those in need, oppressed, and marginalized. Hagar, reassured by the message from the angel, decides to return to Sarah. She calls the spring "Beer-lahai-roi," meaning "The Well of the Living One who sees me." Hagar recognizes God's divine intervention, acknowledging His care for her, even as a marginalized member of society.

Sarah and Hagar's Dynamics. It's Complicated.

Maidservants were common amongst households in ancient societies, subservient to their mistress. Infertility was also seen as a curse viewed with social stigma. Sarah likely felt immense pressure to give birth to a son, deciding to use Hagar as a surrogate mother out of haste.

However, Sarah grew jealous when Hagar became pregnant. Hagar's status grew in importance now, being a wife of Abraham and giving birth to Ishmael. Sarah probably felt threatened by any special attention Hagar received from Abraham or others in the household.

Conflict ensued, and it took divine intervention to resolve the disputes temporarily, but it did not last forever. Hagar and Ishmael were cast out from Abraham's family because Sarah grew too jealous and Hagar too prideful for there to be peace in the home.

Abraham's Role in the Conflict Between Sarah and Hagar.

Abraham indirectly and directly contributed to the dynamics between Sarah and Hagar. He accepted Sarah's proposal to take Hagar as a secondary wife. Although he did not suggest it, he complied when he had the opportunity to refuse Sarah's proposal. He might have been able to predict the conflict if he took Hagar as his concubine, but he did not say no.

He fathered Ishmael, and his treatment of Ishmael may have caused further conflict between Sarah and Hagar. Appearing somewhat passive throughout the story, Abraham does not actively take sides or intervene.

The Expulsion of Hagar and Ishmael.

Sarah decides Hagar and Ishmael threaten Isaac's status as Abraham's heir, telling Abraham to cast them out. Troubled by the request, Abraham prays to God about what he should do.

God assures Abraham, allowing Abraham to cast them out of the family in search of another home. Abraham sees them off with food and water before they head into the wilderness of Beersheba. God likely foresaw the conflict that would continue to occur within Abraham's household. God allowed Abraham, Hagar, and Ishmael to part ways, keeping their families intact.

God's Promise to Hagar and Ishmael.

As Hagar and Ishmael get lost in the wilderness, Hagar despairs, on the brink of dying from dehydration. Hagar gives up hope, but God intervenes, promising that Ishmael will have many descendants. He promises divine protection to sustain them through their journey to find a home, eventually establishing a city and nation. God also provides for their immediate physical needs, revealing a well nearby.

Ishmael and Isaac. Parallel Destinies.

Ishmael and Isaac share the same ancestral roots, sons of Abraham, and therefore receive the same promise - their descendants would be a great nation. They each had distinct covenantal paths. Isaac was the original divine promise of Abraham's heir, but God, in His favour towards Abraham, decides to bless Ishmael as well.

Sean Purcell

Even With The Drama...God's Compassion and Empathy In the Process.

God emphasizes in Genesis Hagar's vulnerable position as a foreigner and maidservant to Sarah. Hagar is first asked to sleep with Abraham by her mistress, Sarah, and then treated poorly as a consequence. God demonstrates his compassion and empathy by protecting Hagar and listening to her cries for help.

Sarah mistreats Hagar, and Hagar holds it against her, growing proud that she conceived and gave birth to a son. If Sarah had treated Hagar well, much of the conflict between the two could have been dissolved. The offset relationship gave Sarah much power to decide how the relationship would be. She chose mistreatment over being a compassionate, empathetic mistress.

The Portrayal of Sarah and Hagar in Later Literature.

Sarah and Hagar's story appears later in the Quran as Sarah and "Hajar." The Quran maintains Hajar as a pious, noble woman with strong faith and resilience. Hajar was written as the mother of Ishmael, a prophet and the father of many Arab nations. Hajar demonstrates trust and devotion to God's provision, displayed in her struggle wandering the desert.

Literary works and adaptions from authors, poets, and playwrights also retell and reimagine the story of Sarah and Hagar. Sarah and Hagar are studied through feminist and sociological analysis, looking at the roles of societal and familial structures and the power dynamics between women during that time. Sculptures, paintings, and other art forms also attempt to display the complexities and emotional depth found in their interactions.

Feminist Theology Found in the Story of Sarah and Hagar.

Power dynamics and the patriarchal system in this story emphasize the women's role in providing heirs as one of the main contributions to her family and community.

Hagar was incredibly vulnerable as a woman and maidservant, subject to Sarah's control and authority. Hagar was used as a surrogate mother because of the extraordinary pressure women felt at the time to provide children for their husbands.

Women's worth depended on their ability to bear children and mother them. The story acts as a source of solidarity and intersectionality, women in their shared struggles against oppression as Hagar experienced during her lifetime.

The Concept of Divine Favour and Election.

While Ishmael was born outside God's plans for Abraham and Sarah, God still favoured Ishmael, promising to be with him and his descendants. Nothing was too complicated for God to handle. The complexities of election and divine favour in Abraham's covenantal lineage (after Ishmael's birth) were made right. Despite their mistake, God can include Ishmael in His plan, carrying out his favour in Abraham's descendants.

The Role of Barrenness in Biblical Narratives.

Barrenness represented challenges to women whom God promised would bear children. Examples include Sarah, Rebekah, Rachel, and Hannah, who initially had trouble providing an heir to their husbands Abraham, Isaac, Jacob, and Eli.

Their season of barrenness was viewed as a test of faith, having to trust that God would provide a child in His divine intervention and timing. God also used barrenness to display His miracles, giving women the ability to conceive and give birth despite natural limitations.

The Symbolism of the Well in Hagar's Story.

In the scene where Hagar cries out in despair, afraid she will die in the desert, God reassures her that He will provide, revealing the location of a well nearby. The well represents a lifeline, giving Hagar what she needs to continue the journey.

God does not guarantee people will experience easy and comfortable conditions. Still, He does promise to provide respite and a way out for weary travellers. The well also demonstrates God's divine revelation and guidance. He won't show every step of the way but promises to be there when His followers need Him most.

The well can be seen as a turning point as Hagar and Ishmael rejuvenate their body with water, believing they will live and make the rest of their journey.

Lessons on Reconciliation and Forgiveness.

Sarah and Hagar's story emphasizes the importance of understanding different perspectives, looking at the struggles and hardship of both Sarah and Hagar. Sarah likely felt despair, disappointment, and inadequacy for not providing Abraham an heir. Hagar likely felt the same as a result of Sarah's harsh treatment. Both had legitimate emotional experiences; both could've fostered empathy for each other, but it led to division instead.

If Sarah recognized she hurt Hagar due to her mistreatment, Hagar would be more open to forgiving and reconciling with Sarah. If Hagar recognized her pride in her ability to conceive and give birth to Ishmael and how it hurt Sarah's relationship with Abraham, Sarah would be more open to forgiving and reconciling with Hagar.

Reconciliation typically begins with the acknowledgment that each other's actions caused intended or unintended consequences.

Sarah and Hagar in Jewish, Christian, and Islamic Traditions.

According to Jewish tradition, Genesis's account of Sarah emphasizes her obedience to God. She is integral to God's promise to make a great nation through Abraham and her descendants.

Sarah is mentioned briefly in Hebrews 11:11-12 in the Hall of Faith. Hebrews states that Sarah's faith she could conceive a child is a great demonstration of trust in God's promise.

In the Quran, Sarah is an honourable, pious woman and the wife of Ibrahim, revered for her faith. Both Sarah and Hagar are honoured in Islamic tradition.

Sarah and Hagar's Legacy in Religious Discourse.

Sarah and Hagar are models of trust and faith that God will come through despite difficult circumstances.

They also demonstrate the complexity of human relationships through family dynamics and societal and gender dynamics. Themes of jealousy, power struggles, reconciliation, and compassion are discussed, specifically navigating societal expectations and interpersonal relationships.

Women's experiences in patriarchal societies, including the agency and gender roles of this story, help determine how women can be empowered in today's religious contexts.

Sarah and Hagar's Story and Theological Significance.

God's redemptive work within human imperfection is displayed in all its complexities in the story of Sarah and Hagar.

Despite the complications between familial and societal dynamics between the two, God can navigate by providing and showing favour to both Sarah and Hagar. He can guide any individual's story no matter how divided their relationships are.

One learns the importance of forgiveness, reconciliation, and compassion and how God uses it to free hearts and minds from bitterness and resentment. Sarah and Hagar also address the gender dynamics and societal realities women face today, emphasizing the importance of empathy for the struggles of others.

Conclusion.

If there is anything you should gather from this chapter, it's that God sees your pain, no matter how miniscule you might think it is. In the same way God recognises Hagar's experience (as a foreigner and maidservant to a harsh mistress), He sees your pain and circumstances, whatever they may be. Nobody is forgotten by God's promises.

God has a heart for the rejected, marginalized, and hurting. Whether it's family, friends, or acquaintances, God loves everyone just as He loves you. Sarah and Hagar may not have resolved all their differences, but that does not mean you cannot. Who might you need to forgive in your life? This could include yourself.

In the next chapter, we will look at another power struggle, this time between two brothers. Jacob and Esau could not be more opposite. A story of favouritism demonstrates the harmful effects of loving one child and disregarding the other. Let's find out what happens and why it's significant to you.

Chapter 8
Jacob and Esau

"The story of Jacob and Esau illustrates the biblical theme of divine election and the unexpected ways in which God works through flawed individuals to fulfil divine purposes."

— Walter Brueggemann

"The older will serve the younger."

— *Genesis 25:23b*

No relationships are more complicated than family. You spend the first 18 years of life with predominantly the same people. You know their quirks, what makes them tick, and their strengths and weaknesses. It's no wonder tensions arise. You are likely very different from each other and still expected to get along. This same dilemma appears in biblical narratives as well.

Genesis closely examines the dynamics of Isaac and Rebekah's relationship with their sons. At the story's beginning, we learn that God prophesies over both Esau and Jacob before they are even born, saying Esau will serve his younger brother, Jacob (very counter to that period).

The eldest son always held the birth right over the younger and typically received the father's blessing, inheriting the patriarchal line. Not so in this story. Rachel convinces her favoured son, Jacob, to impersonate Esau to receive Isaac's blessing. Rebekah has Jacob put fur on his arms to resemble Esau's woolly hair and tells him to present himself before Isaac.

In the narrative, we find out Isaac is blind, unable to see who asks for the blessing. Isaac recognizes Esau's woolly arms when he touches Jacob, but Jacob's voice doesn't sound the same as Esau's. However, Isaac is convinced that it is indeed Esau and imparts a blessing on Jacob. Esau returns from his hunting trip afterwards to find out Isaac has blessed Jacob instead of him. Esau is enraged by Jacob's deception, pledging in his heart to kill Jacob. Rebekah quickly tells Jacob to escape Esau's fury and search for her relative, Laban, in Haran.

Favouritism is displayed throughout the story, showing how divisive it is. What is the moral of the story? Love everyone, regardless of their relationship with you. Recognise everyone. Make them feel like they matter and are included, accepted, and important.

Let's look at Isaac and Rebekah's mistakes of favouritism and how they affected their sons, Jacob and Esau.

Sneaky Versus Unwise. Jacob's Cunning Nature and Esau's Impulsive Nature.

Jacob is strategic and resourceful, bargaining with Esau for a meal in exchange for Esau's birth right. Jacob also demonstrates deceptive tactics, obtaining Isaac's blessing and impersonating Esau with fur, mimicking Esau's woolly arms.

On the other hand, Esau is focused on immediate gratification, giving away his entire birth right simply for a bowl of stew. Esau was spontaneous and emotional, which was displayed in his response to Jacob's trickery, pledging to kill Jacob.

Quality Time. Jacob's Encounter With God At Bethel.

On the run from Esau's vengeance, Jacob travels to Haran to live with his mother Rebekah's brother Laban. On his way, Jacob stops at Bethel, where he dreams about a vivid scene, envisioning a stairway that leads to heaven from earth. He sees angels descending and ascending on the stairway, and God is at the top of the ladder in heaven.

In the dream, Jacob hears God repeating the covenant he made with Abraham and Isaac, assuring Jacob that he would inherit the land of Canaan and find provision. Jacob then woke up, consecrating the place by naming it Bethel, or "House of God."

He anointed a stone pillar at the site with oil, honouring his encounter with God. Jacob's dream transforms his path and direction in life, committing to follow God and tithe a portion of everything he earns. It is the beginning of his spiritual journey.

The Reconciliation of Jacob and Esau.

After spending years away from his family, Jacob returns to Canaan with his new family, household, livestock and belongings. Jacob fears his brother Esau will not receive him well and exact revenge after all the years apart.

Jacob tries to prepare his return by sending servants and gifts ahead to appease Esau. Jacob finally meets Esau, introducing himself again after being separated for 20 years apart. Jacob bows before Esau seven times, afraid that his life and his family may be in the hands of Esau's anger. Esau instead embraces his brother, reconciling and forgiving him and saying there's no debt to be paid for.

Lessons on Family Dynamics and Forgiveness.

The impact of sibling rivalry can affect everyone involved, including those in proximity to the competition. Parents' favouritism plays a major role in developing these rivalries; it is difficult for children to navigate the roles they are expected to play for their parents.

Deception can also create huge rips and tears in relationships. Jacob breached Esau's trust, causing animosity that took time to resolve. Jacob demonstrated humility, bowing down to Esau seven times to display his reverence to his brother. Jacob showed sorrow for mistakes he made in the past in an attempt to reconcile. Esau embraced in response to his humility.

Forgiveness is often healing for both parties involved, leading to lasting resolution and a new relationship.

The Significance of the Birth right and the Blessing.

The birth right and blessing in ancient Near Eastern cultures held significant weight, determining the firstborn son's future to carry on the patriarchal role upon his father's death. At that time, the patriarch was a powerful and important figure within their community. (The birth right also included a double portion of their inheritance).

The blessing was different from the birth right and carried its own weight. The patriarch bestowed it on their chosen heir, imparting divine authority and prosperity to their beloved son.

Bible Basics

It's A Long Way Away. Jacob's Journey to Paddan Aram.

Jacob flees for his life to Paddan Aram, encountering God in a dream at Bethel. He arrives in Paddan Aram, reaches his uncle Laban, and falls in love with Laban's younger daughter, Rachel.

While living with his uncle Laban, Jacob asks Laban to give Rachel's hand in marriage in exchange for seven years of dedicated work. Laban, however, deceives Jacob, providing Rachel's older sister Leah's hand in marriage on the day of the wedding celebration. She is hidden by a veil, so Jacob could not see it was Leah.

Despite Laban's deceit, Jacob and Laban agree for Jacob to work another seven years for Rachel's hand in marriage, building up wealth because everything he does for Laban is blessed by God. However, Laban is manipulative throughout the relationship. After living in Paddan Aram for nearly 20 years, Jacob leaves with Rachel, Leah, their children, servants and livestock to return to Canaan.

Two Wives? Jacob's Marriages and Family Life.

Jacob desired to marry Rachel, the woman he truly loved. Still, Laban secretly offered the older sister Leah on the wedding night, taking advantage of Jacob and his contribution to Laban. It was only after working 14 years in total that Jacob married Rachel.

As expected, the two sisters' relationship had its own conflict. Jacob loved Rachel more than Leah. Leah and Rachel competed by bearing children, even offering their maidservants as surrogate mothers. Leah gave birth to Reuben, Simeon, Levi, Judah Issachar, and Zebulun. Rachel later gives birth to Joseph and Benjamin, dying of birth complications when delivering Benjamin. Bilhah, Rachel's maidservant, also gave birth to Dan and Naphtali, and Zilpah, Leah's maidservant, gave birth to Gad and Asher. Despite the conflict between Jacob's wives, maidservants, and children, Jacob's family was incredibly prosperous. Jacob increased large flocks working for Laban.

WWE. The Wrestling Match at Peniel.

A strange event occurs on Jacob's return to Canaan: a wrestling match between Jacob and another man lasting throughout the night. Although the identity is not given, many biblical scholars interpret that the man was an angel taking on a physical appearance. In contrast, others think it could be a theophany, one of the rare instances God appears in human form.

It is an intense struggle, lasting from dusk till dawn. Jacob persists, forcing the man to bless him. The man decides to take a shot at Jacob's hip, leading to a permanent injury, but Jacob still doesn't let go.

The man finally blesses Jacob, giving him a new name, Israel, "God strives" or "one who struggles with God." After the wrestling match had ended and the man blessed Jacob, Jacob named the site Peniel, "face of God," acknowledging, "I have seen God face to face, and yet my life has been spared."

I Got a New Name. Jacob to Israel.

Jacob's name change to Israel signifies a transformation in his relationship with God. No longer is he a "heal-grabber" or a "supplanter," crafty and deceptive, but he is a wrestler with God and struggler who has come out the other side. Jacob's maturation from a young adolescent to a wise man is now recognized, learning hard-earned lessons from the sweat of his brow. It's through his name, Israel, that his descendants become Israelites. The name's significance implies that the Israelites would struggle with God and overcome.

Bible Basics

We're Brothers Again. Jacob and Esau's Reconciliation.

Jacob is afraid to return to Canaan and see Esau; Esau may still resent Jacob for taking his birth right and blessing through manipulation and deception. As Jacob approaches Canaan, he prays for protection. He takes his own precautions, sending large gifts of livestock ahead to present before Esau to earn his favour.

When Jacob finally approaches Esau, he bows seven times in submission to Esau, expecting revenge if he does not approach the situation carefully. Instead, Esau runs to hug Jacob, expressing affection for his brother and forgiveness. They reconcile in that moment, thankful to see each other again. Jacob provides and insists Esau take his gifts as a tribute of gratitude and favour. Esau accepts them after Jacob's repeated efforts, and they part ways on good terms.

Rachel and Leah and Their Impact on Jacob's Life.

Jacob's relationship with Rachel and Leah was not balanced, contributing to the competition and jealousy between the sisters. Jacob had a deep, profound love for Rachel, favouring his second wife despite her struggle with infertility. Leah, who was caught in the middle of Jacob and Laban, struggled to feel loved by her husband due to his lack of affection towards her. Leah felt the need to contribute to Jacob's heirs so that he would love her as much as he loved Rachel.

God Provides In Jacob's Story.

Although Jacob received the birth right and blessing from Isaac through deception, God intended all along for Jacob to carry out His promises for Abraham, to become a great nation.

Jacob's encounters with God at Bethel and Peniel also show God's constant involvement and divine guidance.

When Jacob fears Esau will kill him upon his return, God protects him. God blesses their encounter, righting the wrongs Jacob committed as a young man and restoring Jacob and Esau's relationship before they say goodbye.

Hold On. Lessons on Perseverance and Transformation in Jacob's Story.

Jacob experiences trials after leaving his family, toiling hard, working long days for his uncle, and waiting 14 years to marry the woman he loves. Laban manipulates and mistreats Jacob throughout their relationship. Still, Jacob endures it because of his love for Rachel and determination to act honourably towards his uncle. Through his struggles, God is at work in Jacob's life, maturing him into a man of God.

Dealing with a deceptive uncle, Jacob likely learned from his mistakes earlier in life. Jacob could realise the brokenness his deception caused his family.

Jacob demonstrates perseverance by wrestling all night against the man in Genesis 32. Jacob does not relent in the match until daybreak, fighting for God's blessing.

Dreams and Visions. Pretty Visual.

God uses Jacob's dream at Bethel to represent the continuation of God's covenant with Abraham. Jacob's dreams provide assurance, telling Jacob that God will directly intervene on his behalf.

The Symbolism of the Ladder in Jacob's Dream.

In Jacob's dream at Bethel, he sees a stairway or ladder leading up to heaven with angels ascending and descending. The ladder is interpreted as the link between heaven and earth, God divinely intervening from heaven to earth through His command of the angels and personal work.

The Portrayal of Jacob In Later Biblical Literature.

Jacob played a central role in the Israelites' history, he was the father of Israel's twelve tribes, and was instrumental in God's promise to Abraham. Jacob is referenced by the prophet Hosea, highlighting his tenacity and perseverance during Jacob's wrestling with God until Jacob receives God's favour and blessings. The Psalms also refers to Jacob in Psalms 105, recounting how God, in His faithfulness, provides for Abraham, Isaac and Jacob. The New Testament mentions Jacob as an ancestor of Jesus Christ. It discusses the blessing Jacob made over Joseph's two sons.

The Theological Implications of Jacob's Story.

Jacob's story demonstrates God's sovereignty and provision, actively engaging in Jacob's life's major and minor details and caring for him despite his flaws. His story demonstrates the power of God's redemption, transforming Jacob from deceptive to resilient, accepting difficult circumstances from an attitude of humility. God gives Jacob a new identity at the end of his transformation process, renaming him to Israel, symbolically redeeming his poor decisions as a young man. The reconciliation and forgiveness between Jacob and Esau also demonstrate that no matter how poor conditions can be between families, God can always restore those relationships.

Jacob and Esau in Jewish, Christian, and Islamic Traditions.

Jacob is portrayed as the father of the twelve tribes of Israel, continuing the lineage of Abraham, and viewed as a patriarch of the Jewish people. Esau is viewed as a poor decision-maker, recklessly selling something as important as a birth right for a meal. Christians recognize Jacob for his perseverance, wrestling with God and difficult circumstances, showing God's favour for those who suffer and endure for him.

Islam views Jacob and Esau as prophets. Jacob is often portrayed as a righteous figure and a prophet displaying faith in God's guidance through his patience and piety. Esau is rarely mentioned in the Qu'ran.

Themes of Reconciliation and Jacob and Esau's Story.

Estrangement and sibling rivalry describe the beginning of Jacob's relationship with Esau. However, after time apart, they grow as men through their experiences. Jacob is met with an unexpected reconciliation when they reunite, the work God did on both their hearts. God healed their wounds over time, ending their story with humility, forgiveness, and restoration.

I'm Going to Find Myself. Lessons on Humility and Self-Discovery.

Although not explicitly mentioned, Jacob likely found out who he was through self-discovery. He travelled to an unknown land, learning to establish his identity separate from his family working hard to provide for himself.

Jacob learned from his mistakes, being apart from his family and suffering from poor decisions. Upon reuniting, Jacob humbles himself before Esau, admitting the wrong he did and seeking restoration. Jacob had to define himself and how he would live without any more parental guidance.

Conclusion.

Jacob and Esau, a story of deception, rivalry, and jealousy, is also a story of acceptance, patience and humility. Jacob began his life like many of us do, caught in circumstances we cannot change but instead learn to adapt to. Whether it's sibling rivalries or personal family dynamics, we all find an identity apart and within our families.

Bible Basics

Early in Jacob's life, he had to learn who he was outside of his family running away. It was challenging not to have his parents and community's support. He had to deal with his uncle Laban's manipulative tactics (which he once used towards his family). He waited 14 years to marry a woman he loved.

Out of God's direction, Laban's poor treatment somehow humbled Jacob, matured him, and turned him into a faithful man. In this chapter's story, we see how God was with Jacob through all those years of struggle, using it to mature him.

What can we learn? Let trials mature you. You may resent it at first. You may not see the point. Just wait. There is an "other side" to all of the mess you call life.

Jacob's patience and persistence led to new relationships, family, reconciliation, and peace. God can give the same peace, love, and favour you are looking for.

In the next chapter, we'll learn about the character Joseph and how he persevered in suffering, faithful as a slave, a prisoner and the second in command of all of Egypt. Joseph is an incredible example of integrity, doing what was right before everyone, forgiving the very people who left him to die: his brothers.

Chapter 9
Joseph

"Joseph is a type of Christ, in whom we see a remarkable foreshadowing of the redemptive work of Jesus. His story is a testament to the sovereignty of God over human affairs."

— Matthew Henry

"Here comes that dreamer!" - Genesis 37:19

If there is anybody in the Bible that started from the bottom and made it to the top, it's Joseph. Sold into slavery by his jealous brothers, falsely accused by his master's wife and sent to prison, to becoming second in command of the entire empire of Egypt, all for interpreting a dream.

As we read Joseph's story, we see his life's ups and downs, remaining faithful to God through it all. His story demonstrates that God allows evil and unfair circumstances to happen in our lives for a purpose. He uses it to mature us, to discipline us, to have a deeper appreciation for His love.

Evil is not the end of the story. God ultimately wins over sin and death.

It's easy to breeze through the characters of the Bible from one to the next. It takes time to appreciate their contribution to God's kingdom. Consider Joseph further. He was likely a slave and a prisoner for a total of approximately 13 years - a long time to be subjugated to orders and treated as a prisoner. Joseph must have been tempted to despair, to think about how wrong his life had gone. However, did he complain about his circumstances?

No.

God rewarded Joseph for patiently waiting and trusting. Remain faithful and patient in trials and tribulations. God's got a plan for you. God's got his hand on you.

From Favoured to Slavery. Joseph Sold.

As a child and a young man, Joseph was the apple of his father Jacob's eye, given a coat of many colours to represent his status. This favoured treatment provoked his brothers to jealousy and animosity.

Joseph made matters worse when he told his family about two separate dreams he had, each marked by his brothers exalting Joseph and bowing down to his authority. Joseph announcing these dreams drove his brothers mad. In their minds, Joseph had crossed the line. They were determined to kill him.

Before they can kill Joseph, the oldest brother, Reuben, convinces his brothers not to kill Joseph but rather throw him into a pit (Reuben planned to rescue him when his brothers left).

Despite Reuben's efforts to save Joseph, Judah proposed they sell Joseph into slavery as a caravan of Ishmaelites crossed their path. Joseph's brothers sell him for a mere twenty pieces of silver. He is then taken to Egypt, and eventually bought as a slave by Potiphar, one of Pharoah's officers.

I Did What? Potiphar's House and False Accusations.

Potiphar is a prominent figure in Egypt, a captain of the guard and an Egyptian officer in Pharoah's court. Over time, Potiphar trusts Joseph, giving him more significant responsibilities after noticing Joseph's success. God blesses Joseph with everything under his management.

Later in the story, Potiphar's wife takes notice of Joseph, trying to seduce him to sleep with her. Joseph resists, remaining faithful to God and his master, Potiphar. When Potiphar's wife cannot convince Joseph to sleep with her, she accuses Joseph as the perpetrator. She convinces Potiphar that Joseph tried to sleep with her, ultimately sending Joseph to prison.

It doesn't seem fair. Joseph was convicted for following his convictions. Where is God in all this? Joseph did what was right, right?

If the story stopped there, it might appear as if God was not there for Joseph. But the story doesn't stop there.

Dream On. Joseph's Interpretation of the Chief Baker and Cupbearer's Dreams.

While in prison, Joseph meets Pharoah's previous chief baker and chief cupbearer. At some point during his imprisonment, Joseph hears both men talking about dreams they had. The chief baker dreams about carrying three baskets with baked goods on his head when birds suddenly eat the food. On the other hand, the chief cupbearer dreams of presenting a cup of freshly squeezed grapes to Pharoah.

Distressed about their dreams, Joseph decides to interpret them, praying for God's divine wisdom. For the chief baker, Joseph tells him that his dream means he will soon be hung and executed by Pharoah. Through the chief cupbearer's dream, Joseph predicts that Pharoah will restore his previous position and allow the cupbearer in his presence again. Both interpretations occur as Joseph mentions.

To the Top. Joseph's Rise to Power and Reconciliation.

After providing an accurate interpretation of his dream, Joseph asks the cupbearer to mention a good word about Joseph, hoping he can be freed from prison.

Sadly, the cupbearer forgets. It isn't until Pharoah has a troubling dream that the cupbearer remembers Joseph. The chief cupbearer recalls to Pharoah that Joseph, a young Hebrew, had interpreted his dream while in prison.

Shortly after, Joseph is brought before Pharoah to interpret his dream. The imagery of Pharoah's dream depicts seven fat cows and seven lean cows, seven healthy ears, and seven withered ears of grain.

Joseph, empowered by God's divine wisdom, tells Pharoah the dream means seven years of prosperity followed by seven years of famine will occur in Egypt and the surrounding areas. After witnessing his faithfulness to God and hearing Joseph's interpretation, Pharoah is so impressed that he makes Joseph second in command in Egypt, answering only to Pharoah.

It's a Nice Coat. The Symbolic Significance of Joseph's Coat.

Joseph's "coat of many colours" symbolized Jacob's favouritism to Joseph, prioritising him over the rest of his brothers. The coat represented status and prestige, separating Joseph from his brothers. The coat symbolises the promise and identity that Joseph would continue to fulfil the covenant between God Abraham, Isaac, and Jacob.

When Joseph is betrayed by his brothers and his robe is torn, it visually shows Joseph's humiliation. The tearing of his coat symbolises the rupture of his family relationships. The coat is taken from Joseph, torn, and dipped in goat's blood to convince Jacob that his favoured son is dead. Jacob is immensely grieved, refusing comfort from his family.

Faithful With Little and Faithful With Much. From Slavery to Leadership.

Joseph's life dramatically changes in a moment. His father's beloved son at a place of honour in the family is now presumed dead, secretly sold into slavery in a foreign land.

Despite his circumstances, Joseph is faithful to the jobs and tasks he is given, demonstrating a willingness and integrity to obey his master Potiphar's requests. He demonstrates leadership in Potiphar's household and in prison, gaining the warden's trust to lead the other prisoners.

As a result of God's favour, Joseph can interpret dreams revealed through prayer. With God's divine wisdom, Jacob interprets Pharoah's dream. Placed second in command of all of Egypt, Joseph played a massive role in the deliverance of the region.

He became a powerful witness of God because he was faithful in the little things, so God trusted him to be faithful with much.

Dreams. Divine Dreams. What Do They Imply?

According to Christianity, Judaism, and Islam, divine dreams are how God provides revelations, guidance, and messages to his followers. They are prophetic, often revealing future events such as the famine in Joseph's dreams or the successive four empires/kingdoms seen in Daniel's dreams.

The dreams represent God's intervention in human affairs as He guides its direction. Dreams in the bible can provide clarity or instructions to follow. They can also be a part of testing and trials, given dreams as guarantees of His promise with unclear interpretations or specific details.

Perfect Timing. The Impact of Joseph's Interpretation and Egypt.

Joseph's prediction of the seven-year famine proved crucial for Egypt's survival and powerful regional influence. Building up storehouses before the famine saved Egypt from starvation and provided Pharoah with abundant land, resources, livestock, and valuable goods.

Surrounding regions also came to Egypt for grain to provide for their families and communities. Egypt gained economic stability and influence within its borders and with surrounding nations. Joseph's interpretation ensured national security - no empires dared to invade Egypt at a time when they thrived economically and militarily.

God Provides. Divine Providence in Joseph's Life.

At the beginning of Joseph's life, Joseph is shown favour by his father, Jacob, with a coat of many colours. God also favours Joseph, divinely protecting Joseph when sold into slavery and imprisoned. God provides Joseph with the ability to interpret dreams, ultimately releasing him from prison.

God fulfilled the prophecy He shared with Joseph as a young man. His brothers bowed down to him in Egypt before they realised it was their brother, Joseph. God provides divine assistance by turning Joseph's negative situations into good ones, allowing Joseph to see his family again and reconcile.

Sean Purcell

What a Time to Be Alive. The Egyptian Context in Joseph's Narrative.

During that period, Egypt represented civilisation, influence, and power - becoming second in command of Egypt was no small task to achieve. The position included responsibility for the lives of all the Egyptians and the surrounding regions.

Egypt had sharp cultural contrasts with Joseph's Hebrew heritage, a polytheistic society with a unique economy, style of dress, social norms, and lifestyle. It would be challenging for Joseph to retain his Hebrew identity in a land of foreign gods and cultures.

Egypt became a symbol and site of refuge and provision during the seven-year famine. It was a lifeline for Egyptians and the surrounding regions, who could not grow and harvest crops. The story of Joseph demonstrates God's involvement in all human affairs, whether polytheistic societies or the Israelites. God is sovereign over all nations.

That Takes Moral Fortitude. Joseph's Character and Virtues.

Joseph displays an unyielding integrity, refusing Potiphar's wife's advances even when he could easily have allowed it. He did not get mad, grumble, or complain when falsely accused. Instead, he became a leader in prison, supporting fellow prisoners and the warden.

His decision to reconcile with his brothers, the family that left him for dead, is a powerful demonstration of forgiveness and love. He saved their lives by providing them with grain despite their attempt to kill him. Joseph exemplifies excellent leadership. Why? Because of his humility to serve others in such a powerful position and be an example for those around him.

Temptation Knocking At His Door. Joseph's Encounters With Moral Choices.

Joseph faced three major tests and temptations in the Bible: the advances of Potiphar's wife, his time in prison and forgiving his brothers. The Bible is not clear how many advances Potiphar's wife made toward Joseph, but the number is significant enough that Potiphar's wife resorted to grabbing him in an attempt to sleep with him. And what does Joseph do? He refuses to oblige and wait around. Instead, he runs away in the opposite direction to avoid sin.

After being thrown into jail for choosing not to sleep with his master's wife, Joseph spends years in prison, indeed tempted to despair. He could've quickly grown bitter at God for being imprisoned for doing the right thing. Joseph is tested in his dealings with his brothers, who left him to die and then traded him away to slavery for an insignificant monetary offer.

What Do Clothes Have to Do With Joseph's Story? A Narrative Device.

Clothing in Joseph's story, specifically the "coat of many colours," acts as a significant narrative device. The coat Jacob gave exclusively to Joseph symbolised Joseph's favoured status in the family, provoking his brother's resentment and jealousy. When Jacob gifted Joseph the goat, Joseph likely wore it as a badge of honour that was a constant reminder to his brothers that he was unique amongst his brothers.

It eventually led to their betrayal, taking his coat and dipping it in goat's blood to prove to their father a wild animal had eaten Jacob's beloved son Joseph. Joseph losing his coat foreshadowed that his future would be filled with new trials, apart from his family and the favoured status he once held.

You Some of Kind of Wise Guy...? Joseph's Traits as a Leader.

Joseph's leadership was fundamental to the Egyptians and the surrounding regions during a crisis. Egypt would have experienced seven years of famine that they likely would not have survived if not for his planning, preparation, and organizational skills.

Joseph stockpiled the grain and resources methodically, distributing storage sites throughout Egypt. When the time came, local communities and cities could travel to these sites for their supply. God gave Joseph divine wisdom to interpret dreams and respond effectively to them.

You Again?! Joseph's Reunion and Reconciliation.

Joseph unexpectedly comes across his brothers travelling to Egypt to stave off starvation for Jacob and his household. Upon recognising his brothers, Joseph does not immediately reveal his identity. He wants first to test his brothers to see if they have changed. Joseph puts valuables in their sacks of grain, accusing them of stealing to test their response. He asks them to prove their word by bringing the other brother they mentioned, Benjamin. Joseph wants to see if his younger brother is still alive.

Joseph struggles to pretend he is not the brother they sold into slavery all those years ago. When Joseph invites them for a meal, he is overwhelmed with emotion, sitting across from his family, likely thinking he never believed he would see them again.

Joseph holds back his feelings until he can retreat to the other room to weep. Joseph finally announces his identity, embracing and forgiving them despite their betrayal. He provides for his whole family to travel and stay in Egypt under Joseph's leadership. This reunion is a beautiful example of God's redemptive plan for His people.

What A Story. Joseph's Narrative and Its Theological Implications.

Even when Joseph's life looked hopeless, God proved His plan is always redemptive, to cause good in the end - even if it takes unexpected turns and twists and is more prolonged than anticipated. Forgiveness and reconciliation take centre stage at Joseph's reunion with his brothers, no longer hurt or confused but glad and grateful that he can see his family again.

This reunion did not happen overnight for Joseph. God worked on his heart, rewarding him with his family again in much better circumstances than when they started. Joseph, among the heroes of the faith, demonstrated faithfulness through adversity. His story foreshadows Christ, resembling Jesus' betrayal, suffering and rise to power.

Time and Place. The Cultural and Historical Context.

Egypt in the ancient Near East was a powerful civilization with an elaborate, administrative system, a well-established religion, and complex social structures. Egypt had a distinct social order separated by differing levels of authority. (Joseph's story in Egypt begins at the bottom of this hierarchy).

Egypt had an expansive, polytheistic religion, worshipping deities reflecting various forms of nature and life. Egypt's economy was predominantly based on agriculture, as many ancient Near Eastern civilizations. Egypt played a central role in diplomacy and trade within the surrounding regions.

Cultural diversity spread throughout Near Eastern societies, thanks to the development of the wheel and roads and a more interconnected world. Joseph's governmental role reflected

Egypt's sophisticated bureaucratic systems that ancient civilizations developed to rule their populace more effectively.

It's Like Joseph Just Knew. Joseph's Interpretation.

God provided Joseph the opportunity to interpret Pharaoh's dream, the most powerful man in Egypt, if not the world at that time. How? He allowed Joseph to be sold into slavery in Egypt and then placed in prison with two servants who would have significant access to Pharoah.

What looked like a curse and a punishment was the stepping stone to Joseph's rise to power. He stood before Pharaoh, interpreting a dream that would forever change his life and the world. It led to his prominent governmental role, his strategic planning and preparation for the famine, and the famine's fulfilment.

Dad? Joseph's Special Relationship With His Father Jacob.

Joseph and Jacob had a special bond, the first son of his favoured wife Rachel. Just as God revealed himself to Jacob at Bethel, God revealed himself to Joseph in a dream. After Joseph's brothers fake Joseph's death, Jacob grieves for Joseph more than he would any other son. Jacob's joy abounds when he finally reunites with Joseph in Egypt.

The Hardest Moral To Get Right? Integrity.

Joseph could have easily obliged to Potiphar's wife's advances. Joseph knew in his heart that it was wrong; not only would he betray his master and commit adultery, he would violate his principles to first marry a woman before having sexual relations. Joseph had the incredible integrity to resist and run in the opposite direction.

Joseph demonstrated integrity throughout his administration, collecting grain and providing for Egypt without cheating anyone. Joseph was fair and honest in his post as Pharoah's second in command.

A Model of Forgiveness and Compassion.

Joseph's display of forgiveness towards his brothers after suffering for years as a slave and prisoner is commendable. Joseph could have quickly imprisoned them and made them suffer the consequences of their decisions.

Instead, he left their fate in God's hands. He saw his brothers were repentant of what they had done. He compassionately reassures them not to be distressed or angry with themselves, for God had sent him to Egypt to save them in advance.

What a story. Joseph views his brothers' betrayal through the lens that everything happens as a part of God's higher plan and purpose.

What Do Others Have to Say? Joseph in the Later Biblical Narrative.

Joseph will be recognized later in the Bible for bringing his father's family to Egypt. Joseph's story sets the stage for Moses' leadership in Exodus, leading the Israelites out of Egypt through the wilderness to the land of Canaan. Joseph's story symbolises salvation, used by God to deliver the Egyptians and surrounding regions from starvation. He is also widely viewed as a role model of godly character, demonstrating faithfulness to God's principles amid temptation. He is a legacy of forgiveness and its redemptive power in individual lives.

Conclusion.

What can we learn from Joseph?

God rewards integrity. Integrity is the highest virtue and the hardest to get right. It means to conduct yourself honestly in all decisions, words, thoughts, or deeds. It's the most authentic reflection of the heart.

Does anybody even have integrity? It sounds too difficult to have!

Integrity develops over time. It requires honesty with ourselves to grow in areas where we know it is easy to compromise. Once we work on our weaknesses, we become more robust and able to handle situations with a pure heart and a clear conscience.

It's commonly assumed lying and cheating to get ahead for your social status, education or career is okay. It's just a tiny lie, right?

No matter how small a secret is, it always grows. Lying becomes easier and easier, and it metastasises. It is detrimental to your soul, mind, even your body.

Look at Joseph's life and consider where integrity got him. It did not work out immediately for Joseph; it actually made his situation worse. But does integrity lead him to? Second in command of Egypt, a leader with a profound impact on millions of people. When faithful with little, God will let you be faithful with much.

In the next chapter, we'll look at the twelve tribes and how they developed from a family into a nation, conquering Canaan. We will see the fulfilment of God's covenant with Abraham to make his descendants a great nation.

Chapter 10
The Twelve Tribes of Israel

"The twelve tribes are integral to the biblical narrative, representing the people of Israel in their journey from slavery to nationhood. Their unity and diversity echo the broader theological themes of the Hebrew Bible."

— **Michael Fishbane**

"Your descendants will be like the dust of the earth..."

— Genesis 13:16

God promised Abraham would be the father of a great nation, and we see that in the development of the 12 tribes. Tribal systems were a common way to identify family ties in the Ancient Near East. We see that the tribal system plays a significant role in unity and division, not only in conquering and settling Canaan but also in the splitting and feuds between the tribes, eventually forming the southern kingdom of Judah and the northern kingdom of Israel.

As we read about the twelve tribes of Israel, we see God's desire for unity amongst His chosen people. Sadly, sin got in the way, pinning them against one another following the ways of the world around them. As a result of their disobedience, God sends foreign countries to conquer and punish Israel and Judah. It ultimately led to the Assyrian and Babylonian exiles. What can we learn from their mistakes? Live out the unity God has called us to have with fellow believers.

You're a Tribe. You're a Tribe. The Formation of the Twelve Tribes.

The twelve tribes of Israel are as follows:

1. Reuben.
2. Simeon.
3. Judah.
4. Dan.
5. Naphtali.
6. Gad.
7. Asher.
8. Issachar.
9. Zebulun.
10. Benjamin
11. Ephraim.
12. Manasseh.

(Jacob's son Levi was not included within the twelve tribes. He and his descendants were set apart as priests of Israel, in charge of conducting religious ceremonies and living amongst the twelve tribes of Israel without an inheritance of their own).

Give Me a Good Word. Jacob's Blessings and Prophecies.

Jacob prophesies over each of his sons with a brief statement, blessing or admonishment of the future.

Bible Basics

1. Reuben: Jacob addresses Reuben's lack of self-control and instability. Reuben forfeited his birth right because he "defiled" his father's bed.
2. Simeon and Levi. Jacob admonishes Simeon and Levi for their acts of violence, warning them against making decisions in their anger. They will be scattered and dispersed within Israel, according to Jacob.
3. Judah. Judah is highly favoured by Jacob, proclaiming that a messianic figure will come from Judah's tribe, namely Christ, as well as a lineage of kings, including David.
4. Zebulun and Issachar. Jacob prophesies that Zebulun and Issachar will experience an abundance of agriculture and trade near the sea.
5. Dan. Dan will act as a judge within Israel, but Jacob also mentions that the tribe is prone to deceit and betrayal, affecting the tribe later.
6. Gad. Gad will be open to their enemies' raids but will defeat them in battle.
7. Asher. Jacob speaks briefly about the Tribe of Asher, predicting their prosperity and abundance in a fertile, fruitful land.
8. Naphtali. Naphtali is compared to a deer set free, emphasising their freedom and agility.
9. Joseph. Jacob blesses Joseph and his two sons with promises of a prosperous, fruitful life and abundant land.
10. Benjamin. Benjamin is compared to a ravenous wolf, demonstrating his courage and strength in battle.

It's a Long Ways Away. The Journey to Becoming the Nation of Israel.

The sons of Jacob, alongside Joseph's two sons, formed the twelve tribes of Israel. Over the course of 400 years, the twelve tribes formed a large, influential group in Egypt, becoming so great that the Egyptians feared they might rebel against their authority. The Egyptians, under Pharoah, then enslave the Israelites, and God hears the cries of His people suffering. God decides to free them and lead them out of Egypt through his spokesperson, Moses.

God establishes a covenant with the Israelites at Mount Sinai, introducing the Ten Commandments and instructing them on how to conduct their civil, moral, and religious life. However, shortly after meeting God at Mount Sinai, the Israelites became idolatrous and complaining, cursed to wander the wilderness as a result of their sins.

When the older generation who sinned passed away, Joshua leads the new generation of Israelites to conquer and settle the land of Canaan. After settling in Canaan, the Israelites fall again for idolatry, and other nations conquer and harass them as God promised they would in Deuteronomy. The Israelites repent and call out for help when they suffer at the hands of their enemies, and God sends judges to rescue the Israelites.

Following the period of the judges, the Israelites demand that God give them a king to be like the nations around them. This ushers in the era of the monarchy, with God introducing Saul as their king before taking his kingdom and giving it to David.

Prove It. The Historical Context And Archaeological Evidence of the Twelve Tribes.

The Israelites' early history is rooted in a semi-nomadic lifestyle, which gives archaeologists fewer materials to evaluate their history. There is more archaeological evidence of Israel's settlement of Canaan however, as archaeologists have found excavation sites in modern-day Israel and Palestine reflecting diverse settlements inhabited during the Iron Age, from 1200-1000 B.C.

Ancient texts, inscriptions and steles record historical events and kings/entities related to the House of David and the Israelites. The Bible provides a background of the twelve tribes' origins, migrations, settlements, and relationships with the surrounding nations. It does not produce outside archaeological or historical documents. Some biblical experts and archaeologists attempt to identify the tribal territories' boundaries during specific periods, but the identifications remain speculative.

So Divided. The Division of Land Among the 12 Tribes of Israel.

In Joshua, it mentions the division of the twelve tribes of Israel and their allocated land by God and the casting of lots.

First, the Levites were to live among the tribes in cities and pasturelands, serving as priests and provided for by Israel's offerings to God.

Second, Joseph received a double portion of his inheritance through Ephraim and Manasseh, prophesied by Jacob and fulfilled by God.

The remaining tribal territories were decided by casting lots, an important decision-making method. Joshua mentions the tribal territories assigned, including pastures, villages, fields, and cities.

Each allotment had unique characteristics, with resources, topography, and geographical features, that resulted in a religious, economic, and social impact on the individual tribes. The original boundaries were likely adjusted over time. The Israelites faced conquerors and fought between tribes throughout their history.

Judge Me. No, Really. The Leadership of Judges in Tribal History.

Once the Israelites settled in Canaan, they repeated cycles of apostasy. In response to their rebellion, God allowed the Israelites to be conquered by foreign powers. The Israelites then cried out to God after realizing their sins, pleading for help. God sent judges to deliver them, who acted as military leaders, spiritual guides, arbiters, and administrators - some of the most notable include Ehud, Deborah, Gideon and Samson.

The judges' cycle occurred over 300-400 years, marked by decentralized leadership with no successor to continue a judge's line. God delivered Israel from the Moabites, the Philistines, and the Canaanites through his appointed judges. The judges acted as spiritual guides, seeking to direct the Israelites back to their moral and religious integrity. The judges were not perfect, however, displaying personal weaknesses in their leadership.

What Does The 12 Tribes Teach About God?

The formation of the twelve tribes fulfilled God's covenant with Abraham to give him a great nation and descendants as numerous as the stars.

The twelve tribes represent God's desire for unity in diversity; each tribe had its own role, land allotment, and identity, yet they were still a unified nation.

God can create cohesiveness out of noncomplementary situations, as displayed in Israel's unity when worshipping God.

The twelve tribes are referenced in the Old Testament and Revelations, envisioning the unity of every tribe, tongue, and nation before God - a foreshadowing of the spiritual unity that will be seen in heaven.

God is All About Unity and Diversity. Lessons from the Tribes of Israel.

Although the tribes of Israel had unique individual characteristics, territories, and identities, they shared a purpose. To worship their God and reflect His nature on earth, a beacon of hope. At its height, the twelve tribes of Israel appreciated their differences, recognising each tribe contributed in a unique way to the nation of Israel.

The tribes also demonstrated mutual support and cooperation in times of crisis and external threats. They showed the importance of loyalty in the difficult times and the times of celebration. They modelled conflict resolution by coming together to address a spiritual or physical crisis electing leaders with moral authority.

The relationships between the twelve tribes of Israel can apply to diverse communities today, offering guidance on creating unity.

Do What Now? The Cultural and Religious Practices of the Twelve Tribes.

All twelve tribes of Israel shared the same monotheistic faith. They used the Tabernacle (which later became the Temple), performed sacrifices and feasts, and celebrated religious festivals like Sukkot (Feast of Tabernacles), Shavuot (Pentecost), and the Passover. The Israelites recognized the role of the Levitical priesthood and their unique contribution to their temple services, sacrifices, and religious rituals. The twelve tribes each had a symbol or banner representing their identity when carrying it into war.

The twelve tribes shared many of the same religious practices, but their distinctive inheritance affected their lifestyle, settlements, and agricultural practices. Each tribe had unique traditions and customs, tribal celebrations, social gatherings, and marriage ceremonies. They ruled each other through a set of tribal councils, elders, and leaders who made decisions on behalf of the community and settled disputes.

Who Are We? The Role of Tribal Identity in Ancient Israel.

Each tribe recognized its ancestral heritage, tracing its lineage to one of the twelve patriarchs of Israel. The territory they inherited affected their economy and culture based on its geographical influence. The tribal identity also created social cohesion and solidarity, affecting communal responsibility, cooperation, and support amongst each other, crucial during their times of need. The tribal identity shared among the Israelites also bolstered military alliances amongst the tribes, fighting against a common enemy.

You? A Priest? Levites and the Significance of the Priesthood.

God called the Levites to serve as priests and caretakers of the Tabernacle first, and later when King Solomon built the temple. The priests acted as intermediaries between the Israelites and God, strictly observing the laws of the Torah and offering sacrifices to God to atone for the sins of His people.

Levites held significant authority in worship ceremonies, observing the holy days, and leading religious festivals. Set apart in Israel, Levites were exempt from inheriting land and guaranteed provision from God through their communities. Priests symbolised holiness and purity, a significant foreshadowing of Christ's role as a High Priest in heaven. Christ is portrayed as an advocate before God the Father, representing the atonement sacrifice He paid for sin.

Lead Me, O Tribal Leader. Tribal Leader's Role In Governing People.

Tribal leaders played a vital role in Israel as judicial authorities, presiding over settled disputes and legal matters and adhering to their laws, traditions, and customs.

Tribal leaders stood up as military leaders in times of war, organising efforts to repel external threats.

They served as spiritual guides, organising and conducting religious ceremonies and acting as an authority on spiritual matters.

Tribal leaders took on the role of representatives in national councils like the Assembly of Israel, deciding on laws, customs, and policies that would affect Israel.

Tribal leaders took special care to preserve tribal identity by teaching the younger generations oral history traditions.

Successors of tribal leaders were typically their descendants, but leaders could be chosen based on merit and charisma and being selected by the tribal assembly.

Tribal leaders were responsible for negotiation and diplomacy amongst tribes and neighbouring nations, collaborating with central authorities like central councils or kings, prophets or judges.

Tribal Alliances. What About Them?

Alliances played a crucial role in the conquest of Canaan.

The Israelites banded against their adversaries until each tribe had territory to settle. The Israelites also formed defensive alliances against common enemies such as the Philistines, Moabites and Ammonites. The tribes formed alliances under leaders like Jephthah, Gideon and Deborah, who demonstrated spiritual leadership and charisma.

Tribal leaders established alliances to solidify their influence, leadership, and power. David, for example, made alliances to consolidate his reign.

The tribes also reaffirmed their faith in God through covenantal and religious alliances, rededicating themselves to God's law. Temporary coalitions were sometimes formed to address a specific issue, disbanding once the objective was achieved or no longer a pressing issue.

Where Else? Tribes' Portrayal in Other Books of the Bible.

In the book of Joshua, the twelve tribes are united, ridding Canaan of its inhabitants as they settle their allotted territories. On the other hand, the book of Judges depicts an unstable cycle of the twelve tribes resorting to idolatry and intermarriage with surrounding nations, causing divine punishment. They cry out to God in repentance after experiencing the consequences of their decisions, delivered by judges after repenting.

In Samuel, the tribes unite to request a king, uniting under King Saul first and later under King David when God strips Saul of his reign. 1 and 2 Kings narrates the downfall of the united monarchy, resulting in a division between the Northern Kingdom of Israel and the Southern Kingdom of Judah.

How To Lead and Govern as a Whole. Lessons from the Tribal System.

The tribal system ruled through decentralized leadership. Most governance occurred at a local level, giving tribes, cities, and towns the freedom to lead their lives as they saw fit. Collaborative decision-making for tribes included assemblies or councils of respected individuals and elders in the community.

The tribal system was adaptable and flexible, fitting the needs for governance within each tribe. A system of checks and balances was in place because multiple tribal leaders decided on governance matters. Tribal leaders played a central role in conflict resolution, acting as case judges and mediators.

The tribal system also recognised the diverse strengths within each tribe, focusing on improving the issues specific to them. Tribal leaders were responsible for cultural preservation, ensuring future generations could recite and remember their tribe's history.

The Tribes And Their Role in Establishing the Monarchy.

Although the tribal system had its benefits for governance, the twelve tribes sought a monarchy. They wanted a centralized leadership, a king they could unite under.

In response to their request, God chooses Saul, the first king of Israel, anointing him through Samuel at Ramah. Saul is not fully accepted as king by all twelve tribes but gains support and acceptance over time from various tribes. While serving as a commander in Saul's army, David of Bethlehem gains fame and recognition because of his military prowess, earning the tribes' approval. This support proves important as King David gains momentum to become king of Judah and later all of Israel. The tribes united under King David and later King Solomon, submitting to their ability to govern, their diplomatic skills, and their ability to create strategic alliances.

Although they were under a centralised monarchy, tribal dynamics played a significant role in governing Israel. The kings still had to work with and earn the approval of tribal leaders and significant authority figures within their community. Following Solomon's reign, it became difficult to unify all tribes under a central leader, leading to the split between the Southern Kingdom and the Northern Kingdom.

Tribes also influenced different figures' succession or ascension to the throne, which was vital to gaining unity under one king.

Why Are We Divided? The Kingdom's Division and Tribes' Exile.

Israel was unfairly burdened with forced labour, heavy taxation and other mistreatment under the reign of Solomon, in part due to the building of the temple and the overreach of power. The Israelites present their grievances before King Solomon's successor, Rehoboam, asking for relief from the demands of Solomon and his administration.

However, Rehoboam foolishly denies their request and threatens to impose even harsher conditions, leading to a split between the ten northern tribes and the southern tribes of Judah and Benjamin.

In 722 BC, Assyria invaded the Northern Kingdom of Israel because of their disobedience and wickedness before God, scattering the people amongst the Assyrian Empire. In 586 BC, the Babylonians invaded the Southern Kingdom of Judah, destroying it and scattering the Israelites in Judah, exiling many to Babylon. After the Israelites in Judah were in exile for 70 years, some were allowed to return to Judah under Nehemiah's leadership and rebuild the walls of Jerusalem.

The Bad Guys. The Assyrian and Babylonian Conquests of the Tribes.

Assyria's conquest of the Northern Kingdom in 722 BC led to the dispersion and exile of its tribes, forced to assimilate within the foreign lands they inhabited. The Israelites intermarried and adopted the culture around them as their distinct tribal identities gradually disappeared. Babylon's conquest of the Southern Kingdom in 586 BC led to exile to Babylon for many Judeans. The Judeans struggled to maintain their cultural distinctiveness, faith, and identity, living within Babylon for a lifetime. The Judeans intentionally sought to preserve their culture and religious practices while far from home.

Some Judeans were granted permission under the Persian emperor Cyrus the Great to return to Jerusalem, rebuild the wall, and establish Jewish life and culture once again.

So You're Telling Me...The Role of the Tribes in Prophetic Literature.

The tribes of Israel are referred to throughout prophetic literature in Isaiah, Amos, and Hosea, for example. They prophesy that God's divine judgment will come upon the Israelites unless they repent while also providing a hopeful image of a time when all the tribes will be restored and reunited, reconciled with God.

Prophets speak on justice and social responsibility within the tribes, condemning the neglect of strangers, orphans, and widows, corruption, exploitation, and oppression of the poor.

The tribes are called to repent, reform their ways, and walk away from false worship and idolatry. Despite invoking the fear of divine judgment, the prophets remind the twelve tribes of promises for a future restoration. The tribes are seen as universal blessings to the rest of the nations, as a part of God's redemptive plan.

And We're Back. The Restoration of the Tribes After the Babylonian Exile.

Babylon conquered the Southern Kingdom of Judah until it was defeated and taken over by the Persian Empire.

Under Cyrus the Great, the Judeans in exile were granted permission to return to Jerusalem. Zerubbabel, a descendant of David, and the priest Joshua lead a group of Judeans to Judah to start rebuilding Jerusalem and the Temple.

They laid the Second Temple's foundation, a great step to restoring their religious practices. The Judeans faced opposition and challenges throughout the building process, causing delays and posting guards to protect them as they built.

Nehemiah, the governor, and Ezra, the scribe, helped introduce renewal and religious reforms focused on adhering to the Torah. The Judeans restored and repopulated the city, organising the city's administration with the help of Nehemiah and building its walls again.

At the End of It All. Tribal Imagery in the Book of Revelation.

Revelation 7:4-8 reveals the number of seals as 12,000 of each of the twelve tribes of Israel, 144,000 of God's servants. The number is symbolic, representing wholeness or completeness rather than the number of tribal members.

Revelation also mentions the New Jerusalem Foundation Gates being inscribed with the twelve apostles' names and the twelve tribes of Israel, likely symbolising the unity and continuity of God's covenant in the Old and New Testament.

Symbolic imagery is used throughout Revelation, using twelve to represent divine governance and completeness, not necessarily directly referring to the 12 tribes.

Israel's restoration and the tribal imagery likely symbolise a united and redeemed church of believers rather than the formation of the twelve tribes of Israel.

The reference to the twelve tribes could demonstrate God's faithfulness from the Old to the New Testament.

To This Day. The Enduring Legacy of The Twelve Tribes In Jewish Tradition.

The twelve tribes are the root of Jewish history, finding their historical claim of Israel in Joshua when they conquered the Canaanites and allotted each tribe a portion.

Tribal symbolism is still used in Jewish religious symbolism, rituals, and liturgy, reminding the Jews of the covenant relationship with God. The twelve tribes of Israel can be found in Jewish symbolic representations, iconography, and Jewish art, using visual symbols or representations.

The Jewish people also recognize the twelve tribes as a symbol of the collective heritage and unity worldwide. Although each tribe has lost its distinct identity over time, it is still a symbol of divine promise and solidarity.

What Happened to Us? "Lost Tribes" In Historical and Popular Discourse.

The exile of the Northern Kingdom in 722 BC led to the Jewish dispersion and loss of tribal identity over time.

However, that has not stopped the pursuit of explaining where each tribe was located and what they were like before and after the exile through theories and legends.

There are limited biblical accounts and historical records to shed light on the issue, leading to significant speculations about each tribe's fate and whereabouts. Theories suggest that the twelve tribes could have dispersed in the Americas, Central Asia, the Middle East, Africa, and the Far East. Some groups and communities maintain religious and cultural legends, practicing particular beliefs, rituals, or customs they believe they descended from one of the lost tribes.

Scholars, missionaries, and explorers also searched for historical evidence that cultures or groups they encountered were part of the lost tribes.

Some communities claim to be descendants of one of the lost tribes, using historical records and genetic studies to back their claims. Lost tribes have also intersected with popular culture and literature, incorporated into documentaries, movies, novels, and fiction.

Conclusion.

Although we do not have concrete evidence of the twelve tribes' historical progressions over time, the Bible abundantly clarifies the importance of diversity and unity in the Old and New Testaments.

The twelve tribes likely differed significantly between each tribe over time. Geography and topography profoundly impact a group's culture and community. Despite their differences, the tribes united throughout their history, as recorded in the Bible, to face external threats, to address issues that affected each tribe and to restore their spiritual foundation.

We learn from the tribes God's heart for all peoples. God blessed the World through His people, extending His relationship to everyone. God loves everyone's culture, background, and ethnicity because He made us that way. God wants us to cele-brate each other's differences, communing together. We can love each other because He first loved us.

In the next chapter, we'll look at some of the covenants God made in Genesis and how important it is to God to fulfil every word He promises. Let's see how He was faithful and continues to be.

Chapter 11
Themes of Covenant in Genesis

"The covenant is an event in the life of a people. It is not merely a mutual promise; it is a divine commitment to a human partner. The covenants in Genesis establish the enduring bond between God and Israel."

— Abraham Joshua Heschel

"I am establishing my covenant with you and your descendants after you."

— Genesis 9:9

"Pinky promise?" It's a phrase most of us learn at some point as kids. It implies a sworn statement to do what we said we'd do or to keep a secret safe. Let's be honest, though, did we do everything we swore as kids? If you're like me, probably not. Most of us think we have integrity, showing commitment under challenging situations. Do we get this character trait perfect? Not like God at least.

As we read through Genesis and the Old Testament, we learn about the Noahic, Abrahamic, Mosaic, and Davidic covenants and how they play a role in God's direction of history. God's favour pours on each of them for their trust in God.

Why does God make covenants with these men? Abraham, Noah, Moses, and David showed incredible faith by trusting God's commands and believing God would bless them. In Hebrews, the Bible discusses that it is impossible to please God without faith. His followers must believe that He rewards those who earnestly seek Him.

After reading each story, we see that God rewards these men for their faith. God wants to bless you with peace, joy, love, righteousness, a clear mind, a renewed spirit, an innocent conscience, and a pure heart. You will see this favour from God in your life if you trust Him to do so. Love God and believe He wants to make life work for your good. If you do, He always will in the end.

The Patriarchs. The Noahic, Abrahamic, and Mosaic Covenants.

God establishes an everlasting covenant with Noah (promising never to flood the Earth again), Abraham (to form a great nation and be a blessing to the World), and Moses and the Israelites (giving them the Ten Commandments and the religious and social laws and regulations found in Deuteronomy).

It Goes Both Ways. God's Faithfulness and Human Responsibility.

God is unwavering in His promises, committing to do as He says He will. Biblical narratives demonstrate this time and time again.

However, human responsibility plays a role when God fulfils His promise. Humans need to obey God's directives and the conditions established within God's covenant to experience His promises.

There is a dynamic of tension and grace throughout the Old Testament; God wants to bless the Israelites, but they often choose to disobey instead of following the conditions of God's covenant. There is tension between God and His people during these times. Yet, God still shows grace by promising His covenant will never be broken and that His people will always have the opportunity to be restored to a relationship with Him.

What's It Got to Do With Us? The Relevance of Covenant Theology in Modern Faith.

The concept of a covenant is the foundation of both the Old and New Testaments. Covenant theology in the Old Testament points to the need for a new covenant, a Saviour, to replace the imperfect sacrifices the Israelites offered in atonement for sins. A new covenant replaces the old covenant. How? Through the life, death, and resurrection of His Son, Jesus Christ.

He Had Many Sons. The Covenantal Promise to Abraham and His Descendants.

The Abrahamic covenant has a profound impact on the New Testament. Christ fulfilled God's promise that Abraham's lineage would bless the whole world. People from all nations experience the blessings promised to Abraham as a result of Jesus' death and resurrection, becoming heirs in the kingdom of God. Christians inherit Abraham's blessings as his spiritual descendants, believing that Christ died for their sins.

The Role of Circumcision in the Abrahamic Covenant.

Circumcision is a visible mark of God's covenant with Abraham and the Israelites. It reminded them of their identity - God's chosen people, separate from the nations around them.

Circumcision carries physical as well as spiritual significance. Paul writes in the New Testament that circumcision of the heart and spirit is more important than a physical act. It involves a heart of faith, obedience, and righteousness. God intended for circumcision to be more a heart matter than a physical act all along.

Cool Mountain. The Law's Revelation and Covenant at Mt. Sinai.

God gives Moses the Ten Commandments and a series of laws at Mt. Sinai, defining the Israelites' relationship with God and each other. It began the formal relationship between God and the Israelites, establishing their moral conduct and guidelines for worship.

At Mount Sinai, God establishes the conditions for His covenant, some of which depend on whether they obey God's commandments. God would bless the Israelites if they obeyed Him, but negative consequences would follow if they rebelled.

Pros and Cons. The Mosaic Covenant's Benefits and Drawbacks.

The Mosaic Covenant gave the Israelites an identity - God's chosen people, marked by unique faith, laws, and customs. It gave a system of atonement and worship, reconciliation with God for any sins committed. Obedience of the Mosaic Covenant led to blessings as well.

However, the Mosaic Covenant could not provide perfection. It constantly required sacrifices to atone for one's sins. It also had a conditional nature for blessings. It depended on whether the Israelites obeyed God's Word or not.

The Israelites experienced the burden of the law, required to follow an extensive list of regulations, rituals, and laws. It was not an easy task by any means. The Mosaic Covenant was temporary, not a permanent solution for humanity's sinful nature. Only through the New Covenant could heart transformation occur.

Bring Out the New. The New Covenant in Prophetic Literature.

Jeremiah, frequently described as the "prophet of the New Covenant," prophesied that God would make a new covenant with His people. He talked about an internal transformation that would take place in believers, writing God's law on human hearts. Jeremiah also talks about the forgiveness of sin and a new relationship with God - no need for intermediaries besides Christ.

Ezekiel also prophesies that God will give future believers a new heart and spirit. The prophets emphasize an internal transformation with the New Covenant, experiencing the forgiveness of sins, empowerment by the Spirit, and a personal relationship with Him.

It Shows God Is...Covenantal Relationships and Their Theological Implications.

God's covenantal relationships exemplify God's steadfastness, showing grace when humanity does not deserve it. Covenantal relationships demonstrate God's desire to provide peace, love, joy, hope, and the fruits of the Spirit (Galatians 5:22-23). God's covenants are focused on redemption, culminating through the cross of Christ and giving salvation to the world.

God's covenant with the Israelites shows God's heart to give them a new identity, assuring them of who they are. God's covenants with Noah, Abraham, Moses, and David provide a central direction to God's intervention in human history. Their covenants ultimately lead to the New Covenant.

Big Words. Fidelity and Commitment. Lessons from Biblical Covenants.

There is a mutual commitment and trust in the biblical covenants, built by seeking God before one's desires. They imply endurance and perseverance to hold on during hardship, knowing God will fulfil His promise. Biblical covenants involve forgiveness and reconciliation, integrity, honesty, and transparency, and maintaining trust by keeping one's word. The covenants are long-term, lasting until a new covenant fulfils the previous one.

Near East Side. The Concept of Covenant in Near Eastern Treaties.

The Near East observed suzerainty and vassal treaties, similar to the Old Testament's biblical covenants. Suzerainty Treaties were agreements between a suzerain and a vassal, a more powerful party and a subordinate ruler or nation. These treaties included conditions like stipulations, protections, and obligations between the suzerain and the vassal. It was a binding agreement emphasizing allegiance between the two (or more) parties.

Ancient treaties structured sections like witnesses to the treaty, the historical prologue of the relationship, laws or stipulations, curses for disobedience, blessings for obedience and obligations. Ancient treaties were often binding by oath, to be witnessed by the gods.

The Dos and Don'ts. The Impact of Covenantal Language on Biblical Ethics.

Covenantal language focuses on the collective responsibility and community God sought to establish through the Israelites. The covenants were meant to exemplify God's perfection to the rest of humanity. It promoted accountability and renewal, emphasising humanity's need to re-establish the relationship by acknowledging wrongdoing and seeking reconciliation for sins.

Covenants in the Biblical Narrative and Their Renewal And Reaffirmation.

The sign of the rainbow was a recurring reminder of the Noahic Covenant that God would never flood the Earth again. God's revelation to Isaac and, later, Jacob confirmed God's covenant with Abraham, continuing from generation to generation. The Mosaic Covenant is renewed most notably in Exodus 24:3-8 when the Israelites rededicate themselves to God's covenant established at Mount Sinai. The Davidic Covenant reaffirmed God's commitment to the Israelites, and specifically David, promising God would establish an eternal kingdom through him. The New Covenant was fulfilled through Jesus' death and resurrection and renewed and reaffirmed through Christianity's communion and repentance.

How Do God's Covenants and Their Themes Compare With Other Religions?

In Islam, the "mithaq" refers to God's contracts or agreements with humanity. One example is God's covenant with Adam, including human accountability and responsibility. Islam also mentions "ahd," a covenant between nations, communities, and individuals.

Hinduism believes in a concept called "dharma." It's not exactly like a biblical covenant, but it shares some of the same elements, like ethical and moral obligations between individuals.

Buddhists use covenants as commitments, following specific practices and moral guidelines, especially by practitioners.

Tribal and indigenous people worldwide have also historically used agreements like covenants between spiritual entities, nature, and people.

Each religion emphasises mutual responsibilities and commitments between two parties, promoting moral and ethical obligations.

What's Covenants Got To Do With It? A Framework for Biblical History.

The nature of covenants demonstrates that God will fulfil them unconditionally (in the long term) and conditionally (in the short term) - depending on the other party's faithfulness to the covenant's conditions. Covenants guide God's interactions with humanity.

Creation is a covenantal framework between God and Adam and Eve, marked by the terms of not eating the forbidden fruit and later being fruitful and multiplying and stewarding the earth.

The Abrahamic Covenant led to the creation of the Israelites; a people destined to be a blessing throughout the World. God's covenant with Israel guides human history.

The Mosaic Covenant affects how God interacts distinctly with the Israelites, following rituals, religious ceremonies, and customs until Jesus provided salvation through his death and resurrection.

Faith and Obedience. How Does it Play a Role in Covenantal Relationships?

A covenantal relationship can only be established by faith. One must believe God will do as He promised, accept the covenant on His terms, and patiently wait for its fulfilment. One must obey God's commands in anticipation of His future promise.

Faith and obedience go hand in hand in a covenant with God, as both parties have mutual commitment and responsibility. God often promises to bless His followers but does not tell them when and where it will happen. It's in the waiting that steadfast faithfulness is displayed. God's only requirement is to wait, be faithful, and be obedient.

Grace. Thank God. The Concept In Covenants and the New Testament.

It is exceedingly good news that the New Covenant replaced the old. The Old Covenant required a constant atonement for one's sin, sacrificing animals to replace their sin.

In the New Covenant, Jesus is the perfect High Priest. He is the symbolic, sacrificial lamb, acting as the complete atonement for all of the world's sins. The Bible shows that Jesus pleads before God the Father on His followers' behalf, reminding God that sin no longer requires sacrifice than his death on the cross. God now gives undeserved, unmerited favour and forgiveness.

Justice, Covenants, and Prophetic Literature.

Prophets such as Micah, Amos, Jeremiah, and Isaiah speak to the Israelites to demonstrate righteousness and justice through their interactions. The prophets often rebuked the Israelites for their blatant neglect of the marginalised and the poor, and for acting corruptly. They call the Israelites to return to God by restoring righteousness, correcting social wrongs and pursuing justice.

The World Will End. That's A Promise. Motifs of Covenants in Apocalyptic Literature.

God makes an everlasting promise to create a new Heaven and a new Earth, prophesying to carry out His vengeance on those who have oppressed and persecuted His people.

The kingdoms, beasts and horns mentioned in Revelation can also be interpreted as nations or powers that fight against God and His covenants through covenantal imagery.

As seen within apocalyptic literature, divine judgment due to disobedience is intended to reflect the consequences of not adhering to a covenant. Covenantal themes also play a role (in apocalyptic literature) when God will usher in a new era of restoration, peace, and righteousness.

It Still Matters Today. Covenantal Themes in Contemporary Theology.

Covenants serve as an ethical framework for living as a Christian, emphasising principles like righteousness, mercy, and justice to navigate different ethical challenges. Ecclesiology, the study of the church, demonstrates God's covenant and relationship with the church throughout its history. God's covenants are reassuring as a lasting, reliable relationship marked by faithfulness in a changing world. It is reassuring to know that God and His promises don't change.

Things Just Aren't the Same. Covenantal Living in Global Challenges.

Covenantal living includes acting out of love and solidarity for global challenges like social injustice, pandemics or climate change. The Christian's mission should be to collaborate on effectively providing sustainable solutions.

Christians should demonstrate justice and equity in treating a diverse world, protecting the poor, needy, marginalized, and vulnerable.

Stewardship of the environment - as reflected in God's covenant with Adam and Eve - still applies today. It should be important for the Christian to protect the environment with sustainable and responsible practices.

God's covenants encourage global solidarity to band together in times of crisis, just as the twelve tribes of Israel did - to provide aid and assistance to those experiencing health emergencies or natural disasters.

Covenantal living encourages cooperation and collaboration across borders, fighting inequality, poverty, and disease in countries with fewer resources to provide for their citizens.

Covenantal living emphasizes the need to be faithful in a changing world where compromise and corruption are common.

Covenantal living should display hope and resilience amidst uncertain times, holding on to promises to provide and support just as God does.

What's the Difference? Covenants and Salvation in Christian Theology.

Covenants provide the precursor and context to salvation, setting the stage for God's ultimate fulfilment through Christ.

The Adamic Covenant (though not explicitly called a covenant) established the need for salvation as Adam and Eve sinned.

The Noahic Covenant demonstrates God's divine grace toward humanity, reflecting what the New Covenant would be like.

The Abrahamic Covenant included the promises that Abraham's descendants would bless all nations, ultimately fulfilled through Christ.

The Mosaic Covenant and the law acted as a tutor, demonstrating what was right from wrong and how much humanity fell short of the perfection God requires.

The Davidic Covenant promised that David's line would inherent an eternal kingdom, fulfilled by Christ and supporting the concept of salvation.

Jeremiah and Ezekiel also prophesied about a new covenant reflecting a close relationship, forgiveness and transformation from God.

Each of these covenants sets the stage for God's salvation, sending His Son to die on the cross as an atonement sacrifice for the whole world.

Conclusion.

God's covenants are a source of hope, a guarantee of His love and sovereignty over our lives.

God's got a plan for your life. Just as God established and fulfilled His covenant with Noah, Abraham, Moses, and David, He can fulfil the promises He made over your life.

We may never know what that promise is until we get there, but we know it is good.

We'll end the chapter with the hopeful passage Romans 8:28. "And we know that in all things God works for the good of those who love him, who have been called according to his purpose." All things. Everything you screwed up, everything you failed royally, no matter what it is, it all can be used for good.

Bible Basics

In the last chapter, we'll examine Genesis and its impact on world religions. Genesis influences contemporary discussion on world religions more than any other book of the Bible. Let's find out why.

Chapter 12
Genesis and Its Influence on World Religions

"Genesis is a point of convergence for religious dialogue, providing a common narrative thread for believers of different faiths. Its themes have the potential to foster understanding and cooperation among diverse religious communities."

— John F. Haught

"In the beginning, God created the heavens and the earth."

— Genesis 1:1

Genesis has affected Judaism, Christianity, Islam and other religions worldwide. From creation to the formation of the Israelites, Genesis directly affects our beliefs, answering questions like: What's our purpose? Why and how do we exist? What's right from wrong? Why? All great questions that Genesis can answer to some degree.

Let's investigate how Genesis has impacted world religions and contemporary debates.

Shared Narratives, Divergent Interpretations. Judaism, Christianity, and Islam.

Judaism, Christianity, and Islam all share the creation story of Adam and Eve, Noah and the Flood, Abraham's covenant, Hagar and Ishmael, and Abraham nearly sacrificing his son. Their interpretations differ, however.

The three religions believe in the creation story but focus on different aspects to draw their theological conclusions. Christianity, for example, often focuses on the Fall of Adam and Eve and the effects of original sin; how it created the need for a Saviour and Redeemer that is found in Christ.

Islam interprets the sin of Adam and Eve as a mistake, a matter of repentance and forgiveness. Christianity, on the other hand, attributes much more weight to Adam and Eve's sin, interpreting it as the cause of the Fall.

According to Jewish tradition, God fulfilled His covenant to Abraham when Israel conquered and settled in the Promised Land. Christianity differs, believing God's fulfilled His promise to Abraham through Jesus Christ. Islam believes that the great nation God promised Abraham was through Ishmael and his sons.

Time to Draw. Genesis in Religious Art and Literature.

Genesis is represented in religious art forms like illuminated manuscripts (medieval art that depicted Genesis' narratives through the use of detailed imagery and vibrant colours), Renaissance art (Michelangelo's frescoes, including "The Creation of Adam" found on the ceiling of the Sistine Chapel), paintings and sculptures (the Tower of Babel, the sacrifice of Isaac, and the

Garden of Eden for example), and stained-glass windows (visual narratives of Genesis found within churches). Religious literature incorporates Genesis in mystical interpretations (symbolic and allegorical), literary works like "East of Eden," poetry (William Blake often uses biblical themes in his poetry), plays and drama, and theological reflections similar to written sermons.

You Believe This, I Believe That. Genesis. A Foundation for Interfaith Dialogue.

Although Judaism, Christianity and Islam significantly differ, they all use Genesis as the foundational text for their holy books. Genesis leads to interfaith dialogue because of the common, shared stories of Adam and Eve, Noah and Abraham.

Each religion recognizes the importance of Abraham and his descendants' contribution to the world. Abraham and other key figures provide a space for interfaith dialogue to discuss the importance of their interactions with God.

Justice and covenantal ethics found in Genesis affect each religion, looking at the consequences of good and bad actions established by God. Family dynamics and social ethics also play a role in interpreting Genesis by Judaism, Christianity and Islam.

Who Are We? The Role of Genesis in Shaping Religious Identity.

Genesis defines creation and God's divine sovereignty over the universe. It points out Adam and Eve's shared ancestry and common heritage to Abraham, found in Judaism, Christianity and Islam.

Judaism, Christianity and Islam each believe they are God's chosen people, descendants of Abraham (whether physically or spiritually). Genesis establishes their ethical values and moral framework, defining human nature and the need for redemption.

Bible Basics

Judaism, Christianity and Islam believe in approaching God with humility and self-awareness, realising humanity falls short of the perfection God requires and asking for forgiveness.

What's Genesis Got To Do With It? Religious Rituals and Practices.

Genesis is used to establish and abide by religious rituals unique to Judaism, Christianity and Islam.

Judaism refers to Genesis to establish the Sabbath, covenantal circumcision and reading Torah portions during liturgical cycles.

In Christianity, Genesis influences Eucharistic theology, referring to the bread and wine taken to remember Christ's death and resurrection, which are related to Genesis' themes of sustenance and sacrifice. Lectionary readings also include Genesis in the liturgical calendar and teach the book as part of their education.

In Islam, the Hajj, or the pilgrimage to Mecca, includes practices often associated with Abrahamic traditions. Islamic prayer practices include references to Genesis and Abraham's lineage in particular.

Ready to Get Schooled? Genesis' Portrayal in Religious Education.

Genesis is traditionally used as the introduction for the Torah, the Bible and the Quran, setting the context and the scene. Religious education seeks to understand the nuances of the biblical narrative from a historical standpoint. Genesis teaches concepts like the divine-human relationship, the fall of humanity, the idea of creation and the nature of God. Moral and ethical lessons play a considerable role in Genesis, looking at right from wrong through each figure's narratives.

Genesis serves as an intersection point between Judaism, Christianity, and Islam, resembling and differing in the details of each story and their theological significance. Education on Genesis also includes applicable devotions and prayers to live a closer relationship with God and reflect Him.

What Does It Say About God? Genesis as a Source of Theological Reflection.

Genesis first proclaims one God, sovereign over His creation with a divine purpose for humanity. He made them in His image (Imago Dei), but humanity fell, creating a propensity to disobey and sever their perfect relationship with God.

Covenant theology looks at God's terms of interacting with humanity, demonstrating His desire to love and bless His followers but requiring them to remain obedient to inherit their covenant's blessings. Theodicy in Genesis addresses the problem of evil amid a world created by a loving and good God. Genesis sets the stage for answering the pertinent question as to why evil exists.

God displays divine revelation and communication throughout Genesis, communicating with Adam and Eve, Noah, and Abraham. Genesis points out the problem of sin and the need for atonement met through sacrifices in the Old Testament and Jesus' sacrifice in the New Testament.

Say What Now? The Concept of Revelation in World Religions.

Judaism considers the Torah God's central revelation to the Jews, including Genesis and the importance of Abraham as their ancestral father.

Christianity views the Old and New Testaments as the divine revelation of God and Genesis as a precursor, setting the stage for Jesus Christ's life and redemption.

Bible Basics

Islam regards the Quran as God's final authority and revelation to humanity. Many of the prophets of the Quran can also be found in Genesis, taken as part of God's total narrative in their religious text.

Each religion shares some of the same figures or prophets that reveal God to humanity as God's chosen messengers. God reveals himself to characters in Genesis through various forms, whether natural phenomena, dreams, visions, or direct communication.

What's That? Genesis as a Narrative Framework For Religious Cosmology.

Genesis provides the account for God's creation: light, sky, land, plants, celestial bodies, animals, and finally, humanity. It emphasises the organisation and structure of creation, how each animal and design has a specific purpose or intent. However, sin also affects the entire created order due to the Fall, causing a broken world marked by dysfunction and death.

Genesis Has Something To Do With It. Religious Art and Architecture.

Religious art is influenced by creation scenes (for example, "The Creation of Adam" on the ceiling of the Sistine Chapel), the fall and redemption (often found in stained glass windows, sculptures, and paintings), Noah's ark (illuminated manuscripts), Abraham and Isaac (paintings from Caravaggio and Rembrandt), and Jacob's ladder (mosaics depicted the ladder from Earth to Heaven with angels ascending and descending).

Religious architecture includes creation-themed architecture (often related to space and the cosmic order), Garden of Eden motifs (like symbolic trees, flowing water, and lush landscapes), ark-shaped structures (inspired by Noah, often shaped to symbolise divine protection and refuge), religious symbols and motifs (rainbow imagery, the serpent, and the tree of life, for example), and covenant themed architecture (using structures or arches to reflect covenantal aspects).

What Else? Religious Traditions Besides Judaism, Christianity, and Islam.

Genesis impacted religious traditions such as Gnosticism - formed during the Hellenistic period - particularly the story of creation, the serpent and Adam and Eve.

The Baha'i Faith believes that figures such as Abraham, Noah and Adam were a part of God's divine progressive revelation.

Kabbalah is a part of Jewish mysticism, drawing inspiration from Genesis for its teachings on mystical aspects such as the Tree of Life and creation.

Mesoamerican religions, including the Maya and the Aztecs, believed in creation myths similar to Genesis' account. Themes such as moral consequences for one's actions and a divine creator shaping humanity bear resemblance with Genesis.

African traditional religions and myths often share ideas on the origins of humanity, creation stories and moral teachings with Genesis.

It's Time to Talk About...Genesis' Impact on Indigenous Religions.

Genesis sets Judaism, Christianity and Islam apart from other religions, but they have similarities, including indigenous religions.

Many indigenous religions believe in a creation story. They also think the divine and spiritual interact with humanity and the natural realm. There is a level of respect for nature and stewardship, going so far as to consider plants, land and animals as sacred entities.

Although Genesis does not teach to worship creation, it emphasises care for God's handiwork. Indigenous religions often include cycles of life and renewal, conducting ceremonies and rituals tied to time, seasons, and life. Ceremonies and rituals connected to what is sacred are also found in Genesis.

Indigenous religions believe in the interconnectedness of all beings seen in Genesis between the Earth, humans and animals found in the beginning of the Garden of Eden.

That's My Space. The Concept of Sacred Space In Religious Traditions.

A sacred space is considered "set apart," holy, or designated for a specific act of worship. God intended the Garden of Eden to be sacred space between God and humanity, having direct communion with Him. It symbolises the ideal environment, being near the divine.

Altars are also frequently used in Genesis, with figures like Abraham or Noah dedicating altars as places of their divine encounter and worship of God. Then, altars acted as sacred spaces connecting the earthly with the divine, typically used for prayers, rituals, and offerings.

Pilgrimages and sacred journeys can be seen in the stories of Abraham, Isaac, and Jacob, which hold significance in religious traditions as a time of testing and faith growing spiritually. Mountains were often considered sacred, like Mount Ararat after the flood and Mount Moriah, where Abraham nearly sacrificed Isaac.

Various religious traditions consider mountains sacred, representing a climb to the divine, going up in elevation, and in a spiritual sense simultaneously.

Word. The Use of Genesis in Religious Sermons and Teachings.

Sermons and teachings of the Bible often focus on Genesis about the Fall and the human condition and how it creates a need for redemption. Teachings on faith and obedience is analysed through the lives of Abraham, Sarah, Noah, and Jacob.

Sermons and teachings often highlight how the old covenants found in Genesis and the Old Testament relate to the New Covenant. Family dynamics and relationships are brought up throughout Genesis and used to teach forgiveness, conflict resolution, and familial love.

Sermons on leadership often discuss Genesis' patriarchs and matriarchs and their obedience to their calling. God's work in human affairs, His protection, and providence can all be taught from stories like the flood and Joseph's rise from slave and prisoner to the leader of a nation.

God Does Care. Genesis as a Guide for Religious Ethics and Social Justice.

Genesis teaches human dignity and equality throughout.

Each individual is made in the image of God. Imago Dei should catalyse treating all people fairly, with love and genuine concern for them, regardless of their social status, race or gender.

The stewardship of creation is emphasized in Genesis 1-3 as God charges Adam with caring for the earth. It argues for ethical and environmental practices and prioritises the planet's well-being.

The stories of Cain and Abel and Joseph's decision to provide for his brothers with grain teach about responsibility for others. Genesis advocates supporting and caring for one another, showing solidarity, generosity, and acts of compassion to those in need. Genesis' account of Sodom and Gomorrah teaches about justice and fairness and that evil cannot go unpunished.

Advocating for justice and stopping senseless evils and atrocities is a noble cause that God wants His followers to be involved in. Ethical decision-making can be discussed through characters like Joseph, Abraham and Sarah, who face difficult circumstances and have to decide between two rights and a wrong.

Wants Versus Needs. The Concept of Divine Providence in World Religions.

Many variations of world religions adhere to the belief that an all-powerful, benevolent God sustains and governs the universe.

Genesis demonstrates divine providence through creation, suggesting His care, intentionality, and purpose for the universe. Covenants symbolize divine guidance, a promise and guarantee that God will be with His follower(s).

Joseph's story demonstrates divine providence that despite his betrayal and adversity, God is at work guiding events for His plan and purpose.

God is the deliverer of Noah, keeping his family safe on the ark during the flood and for Cain as he wanders the earth with a mark that would protect him.

Blessings and promises are mentioned in stories like Abraham's, being told his descendants would bless the world. God demonstrates His provision amid testing in Abraham's story by providing a ram to replace Isaac as the offering at Mount Moriah.

Genesis Impact on Religious Philosophy and Theology.

Religious philosophers and theologians analyse Genesis' creation account to discuss the relationship between the material world and the transcendent God.

Theologians refer to Imago Dei when referring to human dignity and anthropology, the image of God reflected in every human being.

Covenants look at humanity's responsibility before God and the relationship between the two (demonstrated through God's covenant with Noah and Abraham).

Theologians attempting to explain the problem of evil coexisting with an all-powerful, benevolent God often refer to Genesis.

Eschatology and redemption are also briefly hinted at in Genesis when God promises that a descendant of Adam and Eve will redeem humanity.

Good or Bad? Human Nature in Religious Traditions.

Humanity is created originally with a good nature and no propensity to do evil.

However, Adam and Eve still had free will and moral responsibility, which was ultimately displayed in their temptation and fall. Religious traditions believe humanity can choose between right and wrong to discern how their actions will affect God, themselves, and others.

The Fall is interpreted by religious traditions as the source of brokenness for humanity, creating the inclination to do what's wrong and bringing about the need for redemption.

Religious traditions look at the covenantal relationships in Genesis and see humanity's relational nature to connect with the divine. They also look at some of the responsibilities associated with covenantal relationships.

Creation and Evolution. Who Wins? Genesis in Those Religious Discussions.

Genesis records that God created the universe ex nihilo, or out of nothing. The creation account, if taken literally, goes against the belief of the Big Bang Theory that everything resulted from an explosion of highly pressurized atoms forming the universe through billions and millions of years of micro and macroevolution.

According to Genesis, human beings are made in the image of God. According to evolution, God either does not exist or is limited, and human beings are merely an advanced species of the animal kingdom. The six-day creation account in Genesis does not align with the billion years that evolution argues created the earth.

The Fall and original sin do not factor in evolution as in the Bible. Morals and ethics find their roots from other sources, typically seen as social norms of dos and don'ts that have no absolute basis for right and wrong.

Some believe there can be no harmony between faith and science, but if God created the universe, He created the laws and dynamics that govern it. Science should be celebrated as looking at the intricacies of God's creation.

Genesis on Religious Scholarship and Education.

Genesis often serves as the introduction to key narratives and theological concepts taught in Judaism, Christianity and Islam.

It is used in theological reflection and systematic theology and referenced in topics like theodicy, human nature, God's nature, and creation. Scholars use Genesis as a resource to answer everything the Bible directly or indirectly addresses and explain it in a contemporary context.

Unity and Commonality. Lessons from Genesis.

Religions believe creation is a divine act created by a transcendent force governing and sustaining the universe. They recognise that a higher power exists. Stewardship over creation acknowledges the call for humanity to preserve Earth so that future generations can enjoy it.

Most religions advocate for equality and respect, supported by the belief that humanity is made in the image of God. Covenants in Genesis demonstrate the importance of shared commitments to love and respect one another.

Themes of redemption and reconciliation can be found in the stories of Jacob and Esau and Joseph with his brothers, reflecting religion's purpose to change oneself and others around them through inner spiritual work and transformation.

Conclusion.

As you can see, Genesis plays a vital role in the context of the entire Bible. It does what any good introduction for a book should do. Paint the scene, show, don't tell, hook the reader, and set up the story that will follow.

If you'd like to have a great conversation with anyone with religious beliefs, start with origins. Where do they believe we came from? The Big Bang? Creation? Some variation of the two?

Ask their beliefs about philosophical questions like: What's our purpose? Why do we exist? How do we know what's real? What should we do with our lives? Where do our ethics come from?

Bible Basics

You'll find it much more exciting and agreeable than you think. As long you approach with curiosity, respect, and open-mindedness, you're sure to have a good conversation.

The End

Well, that's it! You made it to the end! Way to go. I hope your interest in the Bible has grown and you want to know more about the God who wrote it.

Genesis is all about new beginnings. We see in the lives of each character that God calls them to a higher form of living, stretching their faith and maturing them. He promises to make them wiser, more content, loving, and faithful, blessing them for their faith.

Whether you believe in God or not, the aim of this book was to give you an overview of one of the most colourful and famous stories of all time. Many people have heard about Adam and Eve, Noah's Ark, Joseph and his technicolour coat to name but a few, yet many do not really understand the significance of the stories and how they have shaped religions across the world, across the ages.

I hope that this book has given you a desire to learn more, whether that be to revisit the stories of Genesis with a new

The End

perspective, or simply to pick up a copy of the Bible and start reading.

If you are using the book as a primer for study and revision, then I hope it helps, and if there is anything I can do to support your learning, please feel free to email the team at hello@annuncia tion.press who will reach out to me.

I wish you the very best as you continue your journey of exploration, understanding and faith.

Sean

Printed in Dunstable, United Kingdom